OUTDOORLIFE
HUNTERS
FIELD GUIDE

WE SUPPORT HUNTER EDUCATION

TEXAS PARKS & WILDLIFE

NEVADA DIVISION OF WILDLIFE · Dedicated To Nevada's Wildlife

CREATIVE PUBLISHING international

MINNETONKA, MINNESOTA

Acknowledgements

This <u>Hunter's</u> <u>Field</u> <u>Guide</u> is the result of many hours of consultation and cooperation among experts in the field of Hunter Education and outdoor lore. Special appreciation is expressed to the following individuals who were so instrumental in contributing their knowledge and expertise:

WRITING and DEVELOPMENT
    Steve Hall, Education Director
        Texas Parks and Wildlife
    Les Smith, Outdoor Education Coordinator
        Nevada Division of Wildlife

CONTRIBUTING EDITORS
    Terry Erwin, Hunter Education Coordinator
        Texas Parks and Wildlife Department
    Dr. David M. Knotts, Executive Vice-President
        International Hunter Education Association
    Todd W. Smith, Editor-in-Chief
        Outdoor Life Magazine
    Bob Brown, Executive Editor
        Outdoor Life Magazine
    C. H. Prihoda Jr., M.D.
        American Board of Family Practice
    Col. Matthew M. Rice, M.D., J.D.
        Madigan Army Medical Center, Fort Lewis, WA
    S. Scott Polsky, M.D., FACEP
        Akron, OH
    Jim Carmichel, Shooting Editor
        Outdoor Life Magazine
    Jim Zumbo, Hunting Editor
        Outdoor Life Magazine
    Bill Winke, Contributing Editor, Bowhunting
        Outdoor Life Magazine

PRODUCTION
    Pris Martin, Art Director
        Texas Parks and Wildlife
    Kenneth Helgren, Illustrations and Design
        Texas Parks and Wildlife
    Rohan McFarlane, Design
        Outdoor Life Magazine

Table of Contents

"Only the hunter, imitating the perpetual alertness of the wild animal, for whom everything is danger, sees everything."
—Jose' Ortega y Gasset in "Meditation on Hunting"

. . . .

"A peculiar value in wildlife ethics is that the hunter ordinarily has no gallery to applaud or disapprove of his conduct. Whatever his acts, they are dictated by his own conscience, rather than by a mob of onlookers."
—Aldo Leopold in "A Sand County Almanac"

Hunting Can Bring You A Lifetime of Enjoyment

If you are:

<u>Safe</u> &
<u>Responsible</u>

If you follow the advice found in this book you will learn:

- *How to avoid* a hunting accident
- How to continue the hunting heritage
- Respect for wildlife and wildlife laws
- Respect for the values of non-hunters
- Respect for land, landowners and land users
- How to prepare for hunting and the outdoors

HUNTING –
SAFE and
GETTING SAFER!

Over the last 30 years hunting accidents have drastically decreased, while the number of hunters has increased. Today, hunting is one of the safest outdoor activities you can enjoy.

Look and Compare!

Outdoor Activity	Number of Participants	Annual Injuries	Injuries Per 100,000 Participants
Baseball	33,200,000	404,468	1,218
Basketball	28,200,000	716,182	2,540
Bicycling	64,500,000	604,566	937
Fishing	45,700,000	78,393	172
Football	15,500,000	424,665	2740
Hunting	*15,000,000*	*1,094*	*7*
Swimming	60,300,000	130,286	216
Water Skiing	7,400,000	16,182	219

(These statistics were provided by the National Safety Council, Statistics Unit in Chicago for 1994-95. If you are interested in additional numbers, they can be contacted at 1-800-621-7615, extension 7307. The numbers for hunting are from 1995.)

What makes hunting so safe?

- **Hunting Regulations:** Hunter orange laws or laws restricting loaded firearms in vehicles
- **Hunter Education:** Now required in 49 states and many provinces of Canada (Alaska is currently considering mandatory Hunter Education)

<u>Check</u> <u>Out</u> <u>Hunter</u> <u>Education</u> <u>Requirements</u>
in the area where
you plan to hunt
(listed by "cut-off date")

(Before hunting, be sure to read the
most current hunting regulations of that
particular state, province or territory.)

Alaska
archery req.

Yukon Territory
Voluntary

N.W. Territories
Voluntary

British
Columbia
10-older

Alberta
12-13 &
1st time lic.

Saskatchewan
1st time lic.

Manitoba
All hunters
over 12

Ontario
1st time lic.

Quebec
All hunters
12-17 yrs.
with 18 or over
lic. holder

New
Brunswick
All hunters

Newfoundland
All big game
hunters

Prince Edward Is.
1st time hunters

Nova Scotia
All new hunters

Wash.
1/1/72

Montana
12-17 yrs.

N. Dakota
12/31/61

Minn.
12/31/79

Vt.
1st time lic.

Mass.
15-17 yrs.

Me.
1/1/76

N.H.

Oregon
18-under

Idaho
1/1/66

Wyoming
1/1/66

S. Dakota
16-under

Wis.
1/1/73

Mich.
1/1/60

N.Y.
1st time lic.

14-older

R. I.
1st time lic.

Nevada
1/1/60

Utah
12/31/65

Colorado
1/1/49

Nebraska
1/1/66

Iowa
1/1/67

Ill.
12/31/80

Ohio
1/1/67

Penn.

Conn.
1st time lic.

Calif.
1st time lic.

Ariz.
10-14 yrs.

New
Mexico
under 18

Kansas
7/1/57

Mo.
1/1/67

Ky.
1/1/75

Va.
1st time lic.

N.J.
10-older

Del.
1/1/67

Okla.
1/1/72

Ark.
12/31/68

Tenn.
1/1/69

N. Carolina
1st time lic.

Maryland
7/1/77

W. Va.
1/1/75

Texas
9/2/71

La.
9/1/69

Miss.
8/1/77

Ala.
8/1/77

Ga.
1/1/77

Florida
6/1/75

Hawaii
1st time lic. or
born after
12/31/71

Generally Speaking:

1. States and provinces require the completion
   of a Hunter Education course
2. States and provinces have records of Hunter
   Education graduates
3. All Hunter Education certifications are accepted
   in other states, provinces and territories

Hunter Education - Official Hunter Education cards are accepted in all states and provinces. Contact your local wildlife office for more details.

Alabama – Born on or after 8/1/77

Alaska – Voluntary, Bowhunter required

Arizona – 10-14 years, hunting big game

Arkansas – Born on or after 12/31/68

California – First time license

Colorado – Born on or after 1/1/49

Connecticut – First time license, Bowhunter required

Delaware – Born after 1/1/67

Florida – Born after 6/1/75 hunting on public lands

Georgia – Born on or after 1/1/61

Hawaii – First license or born after 12/31/71

Idaho – Born after 1/1/75, Bowhunter required

Illinois – Born after 1/1/80

Indiana – Born after 12/31/86

Iowa – Born after 1/1/67

Kansas – Born after 7/1/57, Bowhunter required

Kentucky – Born after 1/1/75, Bowhunter required

Louisiana – Born on or after 9/1/69, Bowhunter required

Maine – Born after 1/1/76, Bowhunter required

Maryland – All except those hunting prior to 7/1/77

Massachusetts – 15-17 years of age, Bowhunter required

Michigan – Born after 1/1/60

Minnesota – Born after 12/31/79

Mississippi – Born on or after 1/1/72

Missouri – Born on or after 1/1/67

Montana – 12-17 years of age, Bowhunter required

Nebraska – Born after 1/1/77, Bowhunter required

Nevada – Born after 1/1/60

New Hampshire – 14 years and older

New Jersey – 10 years and older for shotgun and bow, 14 and older for rifle and muzzleloader

New Mexico – Under 18 years

New York – First time license, Bowhunter required

North Carolina – First time license

North Dakota – Born after 12/31/61

Ohio – First time license

Oklahoma – Born on or after 1/1/72

Oregon – 18 years and under

Pennsylvania – Hunter Education or prior license

Rhode Island – First time license, Bowhunter required

South Carolina – Born on or after 6/30/79

South Dakota – Under 16 years, Bowhunter required

Tennessee – Born on or after 1/1/69

Texas – Born on or after 9/2/71

Utah – Born after 12/31/65

Vermont – First time license after 1/1/75

Virginia – First time licenses and 12-15 years

Washington – Born after 1/1/72, Bowhunter required

West Virginia – Born after 1/1/75

Wisconsin – Born on or after 1/1/73

Wyoming – Born on or after 1/1/66

Alberta – First time licenses and 12-13 years

British Columbia – 10 years and older

Manitoba – First time license over 12

New Brunswick – All license Buyers

Newfoundland – All big-Game hunters

N.W. Territories – Voluntary

Nova Scotia – All new hunters, Bowhunter required

Ontario – First time resident license

Prince Edward Is. – First time hunters

Quebec – All hunters, 12-17 yrs. with license holder 18 or older, Bowhunter required

Saskatchewan – First time license

Yukon Territory – Voluntary

Firearm Safety Rules

1. Always Keep The Gun Pointed In A Safe Direction

- Look around and see who or what is around you before pointing your firearm in a <u>safe direction</u>
- Use a carrying position that points the gun in a <u>safe direction</u>
- Unload and secure your gun when crossing an obstacle or difficult terrain.

2. Treat Every Gun As If It's Loaded

Check it yourself every time you handle a firearm

- Open the action when you pick up a gun
- Open the action before passing the gun to another hunter

3. <u>Be</u> <u>Sure</u> of Your Target

& what lies beyond it!

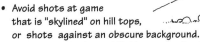

- Avoid shots at game that is "skylined" on hill tops, or shots against an obscure background.
- Best backgrounds are hillsides or dirt banks free of big rocks.
- Identify your animal from tip (nose) to tail before you shoot. *Never* shoot at a sound or movement.

4. Keep Your Finger <u>Off</u> the Trigger

until you're ready to shoot!

- Keep all of your fingers behind the trigger guard
- Get into position & ready before you put your finger on the trigger

Other <u>Important</u> <u>Firearm</u> <u>Safety</u> <u>Rules:</u>

5. Always unload before crossing a ditch, climbing a fence, entering a stand, or encountering an obstacle or when firearm is not in use

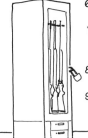

6. Never shoot at a hard, flat surface or water or out of a "safe zone of fire"

7. Never drink alcohol or use drugs before or while shooting and control your emotions when handling firearms

8. Always be sure your action & barrel are clear of obstructions

9. Store hunting arms under lock & in a separate location from locked ammunition

10. Wear hearing and eye protection while shooting

Ammunition

Your
responsibility!

- Use only ammunition specified for your firearm
- Store & carry ammunition in a safe & secure manner
- Follow safe reloading practices

Oh no, Not These!

Avoid These!

High impact, excessive heat or contact with sharp objects can be dangerous to ammunition under certain circumstances.

Ammunition should be:

- Locked up – separate from firearms
- Stored – in original container or ammo box
- Sorted – and stored by caliber or gauge
- Carried – in original container or secure carrier
- Correct – ammunition carried with its firearm
- Round – or soft point <u>only</u> in tubular magazines
- Check condition of ammunition <u>before</u> loading

<u>Common</u> <u>Calibers</u>
of Hunting Rifles

Rimfire Cartridges

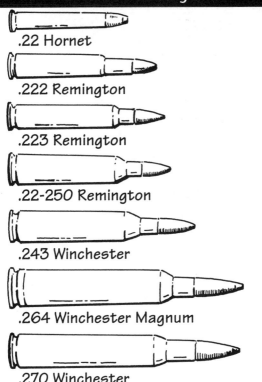

.22 Short

.22 Long Rifle

Centerfire Cartridges

.22 Hornet

.222 Remington

.223 Remington

.22-250 Remington

.243 Winchester

.264 Winchester Magnum

.270 Winchester

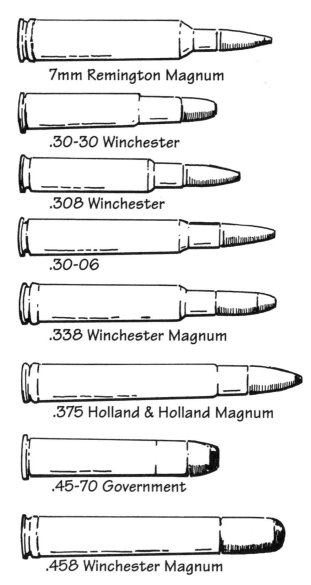

7mm Remington Magnum

.30-30 Winchester

.308 Winchester

.30-06

.338 Winchester Magnum

.375 Holland & Holland Magnum

.45-70 Government

.458 Winchester Magnum

<u>**Make sure**</u> your ammunition is the correct caliber or gauge for your gun.

check the barrel for the caliber or gauge

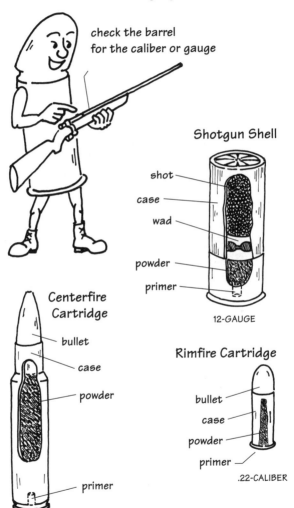

Shotgun Shell

shot
case
wad
powder
primer

12-GAUGE

Centerfire Cartridge

bullet
case
powder
primer

.30-06

Rimfire Cartridge

bullet
case
powder
primer

.22-CALIBER

How A Gun Fires

Cartridge in Chamber

Firing pin strikes and explodes primer
which in turn ignites powder

Gas from burning powder
expands in cartridge

Gas pushes bullet out with force...

Speeding bullet exits barrel...

Bullet and escaping
gases make the 'BANG'

I start
like this

– speed to
the target

...and
end up
like this!

Armor-piercing, full-jacketed

and target-type bullets, -
Do not make good hunting
rounds & are illegal in
some jurisdictions.
Check your local regulations.

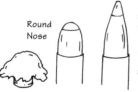

Round
Nose

Spire
Point

Hollow points and
soft points
mushroom on
impact, increasing
shock power.

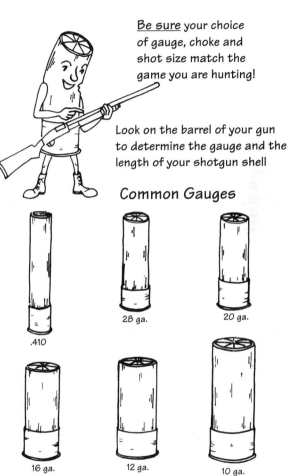

Be sure your choice of gauge, choke and shot size match the game you are hunting!

Look on the barrel of your gun to determine the gauge and the length of your shotgun shell

Common Gauges

.410

28 ga.

20 ga.

16 ga.

12 ga.

10 ga.

Shot comes out of the gun in a pattern determined by the choke.

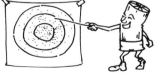

Pattern your gun with various loads

U.S. law requires the use of non-toxic (steel, bismuth, tungsten, etc.) shot while hunting

WATERFOWL!

Shot Identification Chart

Shot Sizes are Relative & Approximate in Scale

Shot No.

9	8½	8	7½	6	5	4	2	1	BB	T	TT
•	•	•	•	•	•	•	•	●	●	●	●
.08	.085	.09	.095	.11	.12	.13	.15	.16	.18	.20	.21

(Diameter in inches)

Buckshot

No. 4	No. 3	No. 2	No. 1	No. 0	No. 00	No. 000
.24	.25	.27	.30	.32	.33	.36

(Diameter in inches)

Check state or provincial regulations to determine legal ammunition.

Shot Size Equivalence: Steel vs. Lead

Lead	6	4	2		
Steel	6-4	2	BB	BBB	T

Steel - lighter, no deformation, narrower pattern doesn't carry as far, shorter shot string

Lead - heavier, flattens and deforms, wider pattern, carries farther, longer shot string

Reloading

Shotgun shells

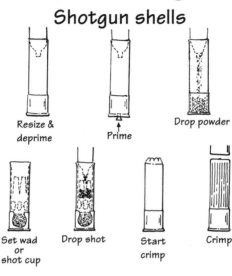

Resize &
deprime

Prime

Drop powder

Set wad
or
shot cup

Drop shot

Start
crimp

Crimp

Rifle & pistol cartridges

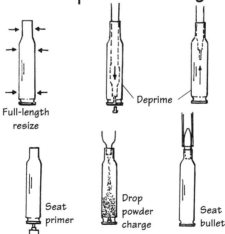

Full-length
resize

Deprime

Deprime

Seat
primer

Drop
powder
charge

Seat
bullet

Get started right

- Work with someone experienced in reloading
- Get the most up-to-date manuals

Organize well

- Keep a clean and orderly bench
- Do one function at a time
- Keep good records

Shotshell Reloader

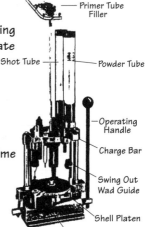

Primer Tube Filler

Shot Tube

Powder Tube

Operating Handle

Charge Bar

Swing Out Wad Guide

Shell Platen

Spent Primer Catcher

Never!

- Smoke while reloading
- Use defective components or parts
- Get sloppy

Use eye protection while reloading

How Cartridges Get Their Names

A hundred years ago, and before, when cartridges were loaded with black powder, different cartridges were commonly identified by both the caliber and the amount of powder loaded in the casing. For example, the .45-70 cartridge tells us that the bullet was .45 caliber and the case was loaded with 70 grains of black powder. Sometimes the weight of the bullet was also included in the name, such as the .45-70-405, which gave shooters a pretty good idea of the power of a given cartridge. With this simple system it was easy for Buffalo Bill and other hunters of his era to know that a .50-90 Sharps cartridge was bigger and more powerful than, say, a .45-75 Winchester. In England, where many rifles and cartridges were made for hunting dangerous game in Africa, the more powerful cartridges were often called "Express" rounds, likening them to the power of a speedy Express train, an example being the once popular .500-450 Express.

When nitro or "smokeless" powder was developed late in the 19th century the old system continued for a while, which is how the .30/30 Winchester and .30/40 Krag were named, but since nitro powders develop much higher pressures and velocities, and because there were also so many different types of nitro powders, the old naming system no longer told shooters much about a cartridge's performance. In England the word nitro was added to indicate which rounds were loaded with the new smokeless powders and the term "Nitro Express," as in .500 Nitro Express, generally indicated that round was even more powerful than the older black powder express cartridges.

In America other naming systems developed, our popular .30/06, for example, means that the round is .30 caliber and introduced in 1906, but that system didn't last. Instead, firearms and ammo makers began giving cartridges individual names, such as .22 Hornet, .220 Swift and .22 Hi-Power, or relating the cartridge to its velocity, such as the .250/3000 Savage, which, as you may guess, is .25 caliber and has a muzzle velocity of 3000 fps. Eventually, though, gun makers came to add their own names to their new cartridges. Which is why we need a cartridge catalog—or personal experience—to know the difference between the .300 H&H, .300 Savage, .300 Weatherby and .300 Winchester cartridges, other than that they are all .30 caliber. When the word "Magnum" is added to the name of a cartridge it usually—but not always—tells us that it is more powerful than other cartridges of the same caliber. Hence we know that the .300 Winchester Magnum has more velocity and energy than the .300 Savage even though the bullets are the same diameter.

Another popular naming system involves a round's percentage! The .22/250 Remington, for example, was born by reducing or "necking down" the .250 Savage case to .22 caliber. Can you guess how the 7mm/308 got its name? Wildcatters—shooters who design their own cartridges—often use this system, which explains wildcatting rounds with names like .22/284 and .30/378 telling us their caliber and parent cartridge.

In America and other English-speaking countries most calibers are expressed in inch decimal fractions, such as .257", .308". On the European Continent, however, calibers are expressed in metric units, and different cartridges are usually designated with a more uniform naming system. The 7x57 Mauser, for instance, tells us that the bullet is 7mm in diameter and that the case length is 57mm. In Germany the ever popular .30/30 is called the 7.62x51R, with the R meaning "rimmed."

Shotgun gauges get their names an entirely different way, with "gauge" traditionally referring to the number of round lead balls of a given diameter required to weigh a pound. Thus "12 gauge" means that 12 lead balls of that particular diameter will weigh a pound. The lone exception is the .410" gauge, which has a .410" bore diameter.

Archery

<u>Your</u> responsibility as an archer or bowhunter

- Use and maintain your bow
  - safely
  - responsibly
  - effectively
- Safely store - carry - use arrows
- Shoot consistently well, within your effective range, in practice and in the field
- Safely use a blind or an elevated stand

Please don't!

<u>Ever</u> dry fire a bow
- Always use an arrow when shooting a bow

<u>Ever</u> be careless with broadheads
- Treat bows & arrows like you would a loaded firearm - carry or store broadheads covered, and always keep them pointed in a safe direction

<u>Ever</u> shoot bent, cracked or broken arrows
- Always check bows and arrows for cracks or separations

<u>Ever</u> hunt from an elevated stand without using a safety harness
- Always strap in, as soon as you get into the stand

<u>Ever</u> carry your hunting gear with you into an elevated stand
- Always use a hauling line to hoist it up after you're safely strapped in

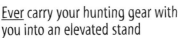

<u>Ever</u> shoot at a sound or target with an obscure background
- Always be sure of your target and what lies beyond it

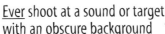

Know your bow... and your arrow too!

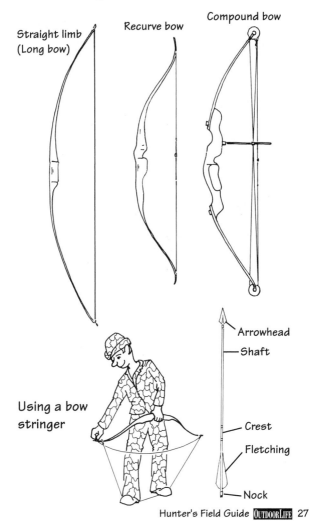

Straight limb (Long bow)

Recurve bow

Compound bow

Using a bow stringer

Arrowhead

Shaft

Crest

Fletching

Nock

Parts of the Compound and Recurve Bows

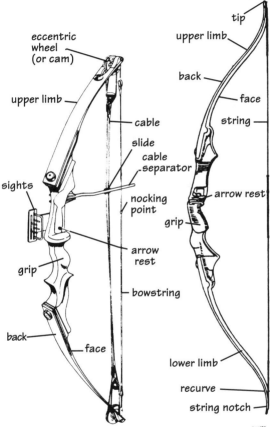

eccentric wheel (or cam)

upper limb

cable

slide

cable separator

sights

nocking point

grip

arrow rest

bowstring

back

face

tip

upper limb

back

face

string

arrow rest

grip

lower limb

recurve

string notch

Store bows horizontally resting on limbs

Crossbows

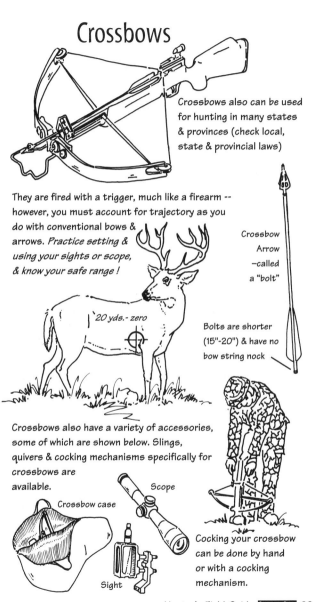

Crossbows also can be used for hunting in many states & provinces (check local, state & provincial laws)

They are fired with a trigger, much like a firearm -- however, you must account for trajectory as you do with conventional bows & arrows. *Practice setting & using your sights or scope, & know your safe range !*

Crossbow Arrow —called a "bolt"

20 yds.- zero

Bolts are shorter (15"-20") & have no bow string nock

Crossbows also have a variety of accessories, some of which are shown below. Slings, quivers & cocking mechanisms specifically for crossbows are available.

Crossbow case

Scope

Sight

Cocking your crossbow can be done by hand or with a cocking mechanism.

Store and carry arrows in a <u>covered</u>, secure fashion

Check bowstrings for breaks and unraveling

Keep points shaving-sharp to be effective. Replace broadheads, or replaceable blades, after shooting in the field

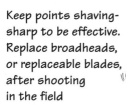

Target Point

Field Point

Blunt tip

Hunting Broadhead

Stance – Draw – Hold
Release – Follow Through

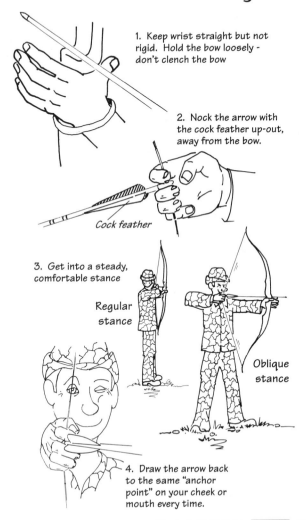

1. Keep wrist straight but not rigid. Hold the bow loosely - don't clench the bow

2. Nock the arrow with the cock feather up-out, away from the bow.

Cock feather

3. Get into a steady, comfortable stance

Regular stance

Oblique stance

4. Draw the arrow back to the same "anchor point" on your cheek or mouth every time.

Practice shooting from a variety of positions and stances

Get out to a 3-D range or play "roving" games to increase your bowhunting skills

If the arrows are hitting consistently in a group away from the bullseye, move the front sights in the opposite direction you want the arrow grouping to move on the target

Release the arrow with a steady motion. Finger gloves, tabs, releases or trigger devices may be used. Check regulations to see what is legal in your hunt area

Always use arm & finger protection

Pace off the distance to determine your effective range

- Get accustomed to your bow
- Learn to shoot consistently well under different conditions
- Get to know your effective range (20-30 yards max for most skilled archers)

Camouflage and Blinds

Camouflage, headnets and face paint should serve to break up the human outline and hide human colors, but never restrict movement or visibility

Ground blinds (wood or brush) should allow you to hide while giving the most visibility, to make sure your shots are safe and effective

- Locate blinds 15-20 yards off game trails to avoid detection
- Contoured edges and curves blend better than square edges
- Avoid cutting "live" material. It may be illegal and green material will quickly brown
- Make the blind big enough to cover your form and movement
- Set up blinds at higher elevations than where you expect to see game animals
- Pit blinds are illegal in some areas. If you dig a pit blind, restore it when you are finished hunting
- Construct your blind so no part of the bow or arrow comes in contact with it while you are shooting

- **Completely** camouflage yourself - look for any telltale clothing, jewelry or skin showing through

- **Never** give the signal that you are game:
  - Never wear or carry anything that is the same color as the animal you're hunting
  - Wear orange or another bright, unnatural color, while approaching and leaving your hunt area
  - Put some bright cloth or tape on your animal while field dressing it or carrying it from the field
  - Never make the call of the animal being hunted (tom turkey, buck deer) when there are other hunters in the area
  - When another hunter approaches, call out in a normal voice to let him or her know you are there. Don't shout or whistle, and never make an animal call
  - Make sure you can see clearly in all directions so you can see approaching people or game, or make sure you are protected in any blind spots
  - Be sure of your shot, _clearly identify_ your target and make sure the shot is clear and safe

Stands

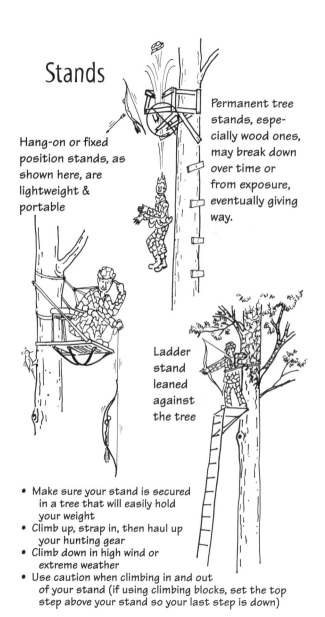

Hang-on or fixed position stands, as shown here, are lightweight & portable

Permanent tree stands, especially wood ones, may break down over time or from exposure, eventually giving way.

Ladder stand leaned against the tree

- Make sure your stand is secured in a tree that will easily hold your weight
- Climb up, strap in, then haul up your hunting gear
- Climb down in high wind or extreme weather
- Use caution when climbing in and out of your stand (if using climbing blocks, set the top step above your stand so your last step is down)

Tree Stand <u>Advantages</u>

- Better field of view
- Scent of hunter is higher
- Hunter is above animal's
    field of vision
- Hunter is not moving around
    in the woods, interfering
    with other hunters
- Shots entering high and exiting
    low leave a better blood
    trail and aid in recovery

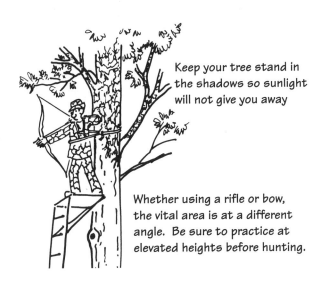

Keep your tree stand in
the shadows so sunlight
will not give you away

Whether using a rifle or bow,
the vital area is at a different
angle. Be sure to practice at
elevated heights before hunting.

Keep the prevailing wind in mind when selecting
a location for your stand. You never want the
wind blowing past you toward game or trails.

Selecting Your Hunting Spot

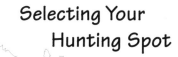

<u>Look for signs</u>
from the animal you
are hunting - favorite
feeding areas, wallows,
watering areas, travel
paths, tracks, scrapes
or droppings

Field Safety

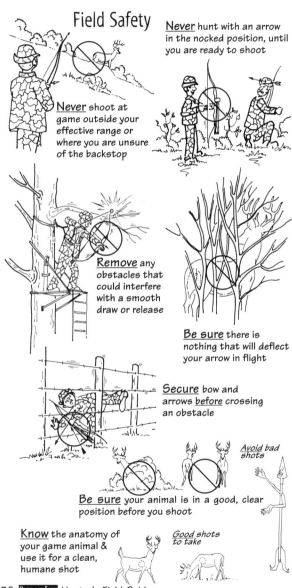

Never shoot at game outside your effective range or where you are unsure of the backstop

Never hunt with an arrow in the nocked position, until you are ready to shoot

Remove any obstacles that could interfere with a smooth draw or release

Be sure there is nothing that will deflect your arrow in flight

Secure bow and arrows **before** crossing an obstacle

Avoid bad shots

Be sure your animal is in a good, clear position before you shoot

Know the anatomy of your game animal & use it for a clean, humane shot

Good shots to take

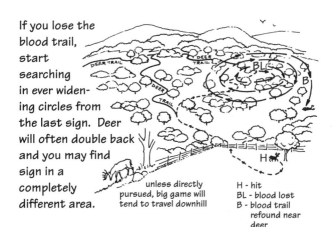

If you lose the blood trail, start searching in ever widening circles from the last sign. Deer will often double back and you may find sign in a completely different area.

unless directly pursued, big game will tend to travel downhill

H - hit
BL - blood lost
B - blood trail refound near deer

If the Deer Runs Off When Hit

<u>WAIT!</u>

for at least 1/2 to 1 hour if possible

Hits outside the heart/lung area require a longer wait—2-3 hours is a good standard.

Then begin blood trailing the animal using these techniques:

Bend down • Kneel down • Look closely

You have the <u>responsibility</u> to do your best to recover every animal you hit.

Take a compass bearing on the direction you last saw the animal go

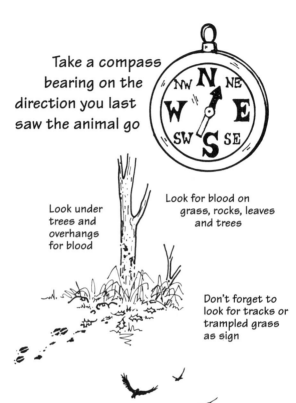

Look under trees and overhangs for blood

Look for blood on grass, rocks, leaves and trees

Don't forget to look for tracks or trampled grass as sign

Carrion eaters, magpies, ravens or vultures may give away a dead animal's position

Mark sign as you find it to get a line-of-sight perspective—
Never give up on a blood trail until you've made every effort to find the next drop.
Be sure to retrieve flagging tape if you have used it to mark a trail.

OUTDOORLIFE

Bowhunting Expert Bill Winke on:

Step-by-Step
Bow Tuning

For maximum accuracy, your arrow has to fly straight, with the tail (or nock) perfectly following the tip. Otherwise, the arrow will veer off-line, which ruins consistency. This step-by-step guide will simplify the process of tuning a bow.

Initial Set-Up:

1. The point at which the arrow attaches to the string should be placed 1/4 inch above the bow's threaded cushion plunger hole for release shooters and 3/8 inch above for finger shooters.
2. Adjust the rest up and down until the arrow crosses the center of the cushion plunger hole. Horizontally, the arrow should line up perfectly with the string (parallel to the bow's stabilizer when seen from above) for a release aid, and pointing just slightly outside this line for a finger release.
3. Arrow stiffness affects your ability to achieve good arrow flight. Make sure the arrow you're shooting is correctly spined for your bow's draw weight and draw length. Your local archery dealer can help you determine if your arrows are adequate.

Paper Tuning:

1. Stand 10 feet from a piece of paper (freezer paper works well) held taut by a picture frame or a cardboard box with the bottom cut out. With field points installed, shoot arrows through the paper, paying particular attention to the pattern of the tear. Your goal is a perfect bullet-hole broken only by short rips made by your arrow's fletching.
2. Refer to the table presented on the next page to determine how to correct any paper tears that you find.
3. Improper shooting form can also cause paper tears. Make sure to spend time practicing good form with your bow before you try to tune it.

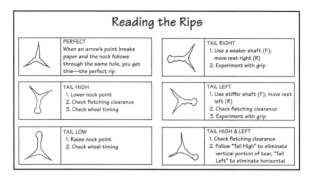

Reading the Rips

PERFECT
When an arrow's point breaks paper and the nock follows through the same hole, you get this—the perfect rip

TAIL RIGHT
1. Use a weaker shaft (F); move rest right (R)
2. Experiment with grip

TAIL HIGH
1. Lower nock point
2. Check fletching clearance
3. Check wheel timing

TAIL LEFT
1. Use stiffer shaft (F); move rest left (R)
2. Check fletching clearance
3. Experiment with grip

TAIL LOW
1. Raise nock point
2. Check wheel timing

TAIL HIGH & LEFT
1. Check fletching clearance
2. Follow "Tail High" to eliminate vertical portion of tear, "Tail Left" to eliminate horizontal

4. If you can't eliminate poor arrow flight after trying all the techniques outlined here, ask for help from an experienced archer or an archery shop operator.

Fletching Contact with the Rest:

Contact between your arrow rest and the fletching on your arrows is the most common cause of poor arrow flight. A different rest style may offer better clearance, but try rotating your arrow nocks first.

The position of your nocks affects the way the fletchings slip through, or around, the rest. If your nocks are glued in place (as opposed to being turnable), you will have to cut them off, clean the arrow's nock taper and glue another on at what you think is the right rotation. Repeat until your contact problems go away.

Fine-Tuning Hunting Arrows:

For maximum accuracy with hunting arrows, the broadhead has to line up perfectly with the arrow shaft. Construct a simple fixture so you can turn your arrows while comparing the broadhead's point to a fixed reference. If the point doesn't remain perfectly stationary as the arrow turns, set it aside. Use only those arrows for which the broadhead turns true.

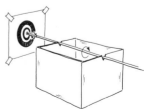

If you need to adjust a broadhead to bring it inline with the shaft, heat the end of the arrow (where the insert is installed) with a small LP torch and nudge the tip gently in the direction it must go to line up.

Black Powder

Your responsibilities with black powder

- Safely store and handle black powder or Pyrodex
- Handle guns in a safe and responsible manner
- Store firearms and ammunition in a safe and secure manner
- Safely load and fire muzzleloading firearms
- Safely unload or discharge muzzleloading firearms
- Properly clean and maintain firearms
- Use eye and ear protection
- Remember that the _effective_ _range_ of most muzzleloaders is only 75-100 yards (150 yards for In-line ignition muzzleloaders)

Boy, Oh Boy - <u>Don't</u> Do These!!!

<u>Never</u> expose black powder to open flame

<u>Never</u> store black powder in steel, iron, plastic or other material that can spark

<u>Never</u> blow down the barrel of a gun

<u>Never</u> pour powder directly from the flask or horn into the barrel

<u>Never</u> use smokeless powder in a muzzleloader

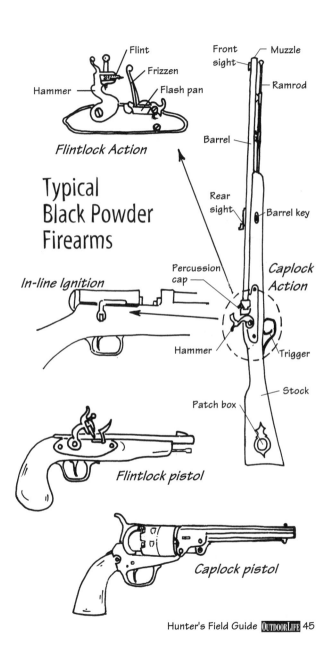

Flint

Frizzen

Hammer

Flash pan

Flintlock Action

Front sight

Muzzle

Ramrod

Barrel

Rear sight

Barrel key

Typical Black Powder Firearms

Caplock Action

In-line Ignition

Percussion cap

Hammer

Trigger

Stock

Patch box

Flintlock pistol

Caplock pistol

Muzzleloading Accessories

Black Powder

Designation	Grain	Use
FG	coarse	cannons, .75 cal. or larger
FFG	medium	.50-.75 cal., 20-12 ga.
FFFG	fine	under .50 cal., under 20 ga.
FFFFG	very fine	priming powder for flintlocks only

Pyrodex - Synthetic substitute which may be used
in equal amounts for black powder
("RS" grade for firearms .50 cal. &
above, including shotguns;
"P" grade for firearms under .50 cal.)

Black powder or Pyrodex <u>only</u> in muzzleloading firearms

Loading a Muzzleloader

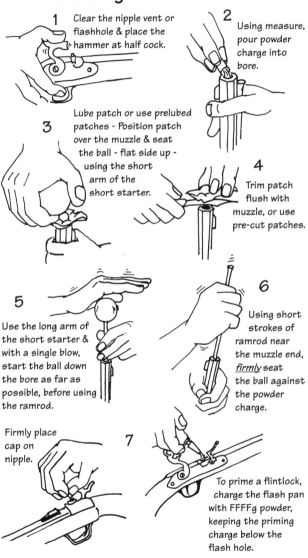

1 Clear the nipple vent or flashhole & place the hammer at half cock.

2 Using measure, pour powder charge into bore.

3 Lube patch or use prelubed patches - Position patch over the muzzle & seat the ball - flat side up - using the short arm of the short starter.

4 Trim patch flush with muzzle, or use pre-cut patches.

5 Use the long arm of the short starter & with a single blow, start the ball down the bore as far as possible, before using the ramrod.

6 Using short strokes of ramrod near the muzzle end, _firmly_ seat the ball against the powder charge.

7 Firmly place cap on nipple.

To prime a flintlock, charge the flash pan with FFFFg powder, keeping the priming charge below the flash hole.

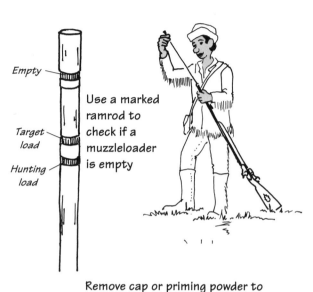

Empty

Target load

Hunting load

Use a marked ramrod to check if a muzzleloader is empty

Remove cap or priming powder to <u>safely</u> and <u>legally</u> unload a muzzleloader for transportation in a vehicle or for crossing an obstacle.

Cap

Priming powder

CO^2 discharger

Use a CO^2 ball discharger (blows the charge out with a "blast" of CO^2) to discharge a misfire or improperly loaded charge from a muzzleloader.

Cleaning a Muzzleloader

Black powder is <u>very</u> <u>corrosive</u> and guns require cleaning after each day's use.

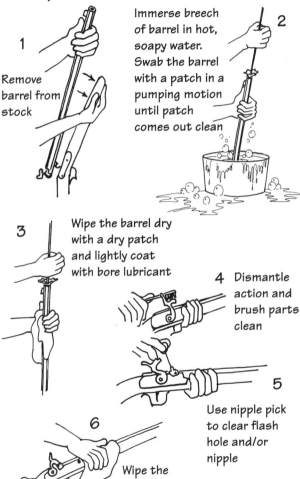

1 Remove barrel from stock

2 Immerse breech of barrel in hot, soapy water. Swab the barrel with a patch in a pumping motion until patch comes out clean

3 Wipe the barrel dry with a dry patch and lightly coat with bore lubricant

4 Dismantle action and brush parts clean

5 Use nipple pick to clear flash hole and/or nipple

6 Wipe the gun down and reassemble

Field Safety

<u>Remove</u> cap or priming powder to "unload" the muzzleloader before crossing an obstacle or rough terrain. Lay gun on ground before crossing

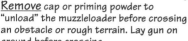

<u>Be sure</u> of your target and what lies beyond it

<u>Store</u> powder and caps safely away from open flame, heat and sparks

<u>Be sure</u> to remove the ramrod before firing

<u>Be careful</u> not to double charge your gun

<u>Be sure</u> you seat the ball completely, with no air space between the ball and the powder

<u>Always</u> wear eye and ear protection when loading and firing any firearm, especially muzzleloaders

OUTDOORLIFE

Shooting Editor Jim Carmichel on:

Black-Powder Ballistics

Because of their relatively low velocity, muzzleloading rifles do not have as much downrange energy, or "knockdown powder," as modern centerfire rifles. Also, the round lead balls tend to lose velocity and energy rather quickly, and their trajectories are not nearly as "flat" as those of modern centerfire rifles firing pointed bullets at higher velocities. These two tables show the trajectories, velocities and energy levels of four popular ML (muzzle-loader) calibers loaded with round lead bullets to low, medium and high velocities. Individual ML rifles and different barrel lengths may yield somewhat different velocities than shown here, but these give a close idea. As a general rule, rifles with longer barrels have higher velocities with a given powder charge than shorter barrels.

The trajectory table will help you understand why it is difficult to hit even large targets at distances beyond 125 yards. That's why smart ML hunters will sight-in their rifles to hit "dead-on" at 75 yards (the approximate range at which most deer are bagged) and always try to get as close to the target as possible. Skilled stalking is part of the fun of hunting with a muzzleloading rifle!

Trajectory Path of Black Powder Bullet

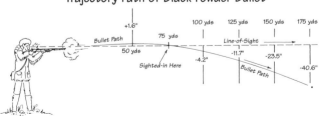

How to Use the Trajectory Chart

Numbers marked (+) show the distance—in inches—
the bullet will hit above the line of sight when your rifle is sighted-in at
75 yards. Numbers marked (-) show how much the bullet has dropped
below where you aim at the distances shown.

BLACK POWDER TRAJECTORY CHART (Sighted-in at 75 yds.)

CALIBER	CHARGE in grains of FFFg Black Powder	50 yds	75 yds	100 yds	125 yds	150 yds	175 yds	200 yds
				Drop of bullet shown in inches				
.36	30	+ 1.6	0	- 4.2	- 11.7	- 23.5	- 40.6	- 64.2
.36	40	+ 1.5	0	- 3.2	- 9.2	- 18.7	- 32.6	- 52.0
.36	60	+ .7	0	- 2.3	- 6.8	- 14.1	- 25.0	- 40.4
.40	40	+ 1.6	0	- 4.2	- 11.7	- 23.3	- 39.9	- 62.5
.40	50	+ 1.1	0	- 3.1	- 8.8	- 18.7	- 30.9	- 48.9
.40	80	+ .7	0	- 2.1	- 6.3	- 14.1	- 22.9	- 36.9
.45	40	+ 1.4	0	- 3.7	- 10.3	- 20.4	- 34.8	- 54.3
.45	50	+ 1.1	0	- 3.1	- 8.6	- 17.2	- 29.6	- 46.5
.45	85	+4.5	0	- 1.8	- 5.3	- 11.0	- 19.3	- 31.1
.50	50	+ 1.2	0	- 3.3	- 9.3	- 18.4	- 31.4	- 48.8
.50	70	+ .9	0	- 2.6	- 7.5	- 15.0	- 25.8	- 40.4
.50	90	+ .6	0	- 2.0	- 5.7	- 11.6	- 20.3	- 32.2

Firearms -
Rifles, Shotguns, & Handguns

<u>Your</u> Responsibility with Firearms

- Follow safe gun-handling rules
- Safely store firearms and ammunition separately
- Shoot only at targets and legal game
- Clean up after shooting
- Become proficient with hunting arms
- Safely and efficiently operate firearms
- Take only safe, sure shots - never guess or take chances

Always wear eye and ear protection while shooting firearms

It makes one shudder...

hunter swinging on game, shoots victim - horseplay with a gun - victim moves into the line of fire - shooting from a vehicle - shooter unsure of backstop - mistaken for game - loaded firearm in a vehicle - unsafe crossing of an obstacle - unsafe loading/unloading - unsecured gun rest - obstruction in the barrel - defective firearm or ammunition - trigger caught on an object - shooter stumbled and fell - victim out of sight.

These are the <u>major causes</u> of most accidents.

<u>Follow These Rules</u> -
and you will never cause accidents

- **Always keep the gun pointed** in a safe direction

- **Treat every gun as if it's loaded** Check it yourself every time you handle a firearm

- **Be sure of your target** and what lies beyond it

- **Keep your finger off** the trigger - until you are ready to shoot

Choose the Gun . . .

- You can comfortably carry and shoot

- That has recoil you can handle without throwing your shooting off

- That is powerful enough to effectively take the animal you are hunting

- That provides the ballistics, range and trajectory you need for hunting

- That allows you to confidently shoot and hit what you're aiming at

Your gun should fit so that the butt rests in the crook of your elbow and your finger reaches the trigger (best to be fitted by your gunsmith)

How Far Does A Bullet Travel?

Type	0	1 Mile	2 Miles	3 Miles
.22 Short				
22 LRHV				
.22 Win. Mag.				
.222				
.243				
.270				
7 MM Mag.				
.30-30				
.30-06				
.300 Sav.				
.300 Win. Mag.				
.308				
.338				
.35 Rem.				
45-70				

Source: NSSF / SAAMI

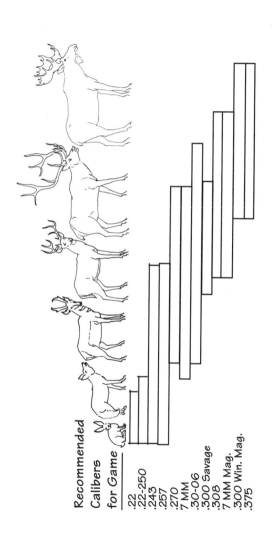

Recommended
Calibers
for Game

.22
.22-250
.243
.257
.270
7 MM
.30-06
.300 Savage
.308
7 MM Mag.
.300 Win. Mag.
.375

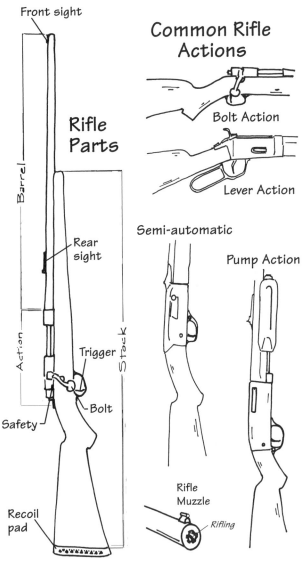

Front sight

Rifle Parts

Barrel

Rear sight

Action

Stock

Trigger

Bolt

Safety

Recoil pad

Common Rifle Actions

Bolt Action

Lever Action

Semi-automatic

Pump Action

Rifle Muzzle

Rifling

Common Shotgun Actions

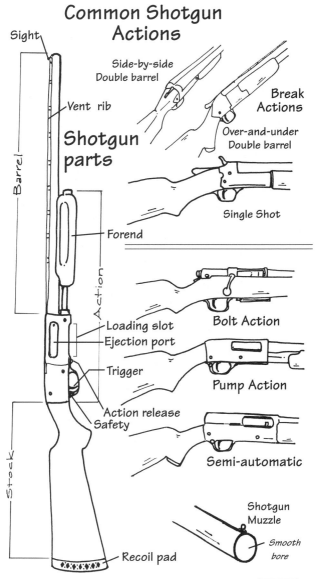

Sight

Vent rib

Shotgun parts

Barrel

Side-by-side
Double barrel

Break
Actions

Over-and-under
Double barrel

Single Shot

Forend

Action

Loading slot

Ejection port

Trigger

Action release

Safety

Stock

Bolt Action

Pump Action

Semi-automatic

Shotgun
Muzzle

Smooth
bore

Recoil pad

Learn how to operate your firearm <u>before</u> going shooting

- Have someone experienced in the use of your firearm show you how to operate and maintain it
- Disassemble, clean and reassemble your firearm
- Work the action with dummy ammunition
- Load live ammunition only at the range or while hunting
- Always keep your firearm pointed in a safe direction

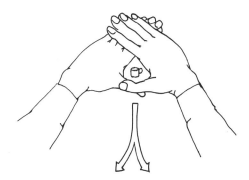

Finding Your Dominant Eye

1. Face an object about 10 feet (3.04 m) away
2. Extend your arms straight out in front of you
3. Form a small triangle by overlapping your hands
4. Look through the triangle with both eyes
5. Focus on the object
6. Bring the triangle toward your eyes, while keeping the object in focus at all times
7. To keep the object in sight, the triangle will move toward your dominant eye

Field Shooting Positions

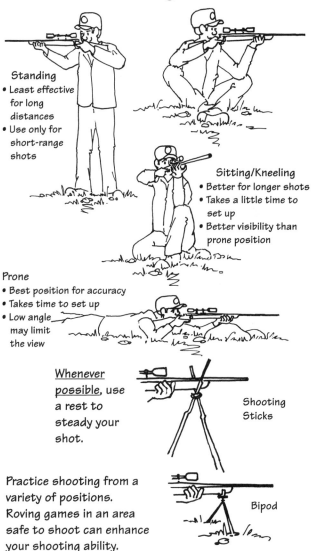

Standing
- Least effective for long distances
- Use only for short-range shots

Sitting/Kneeling
- Better for longer shots
- Takes a little time to set up
- Better visibility than prone position

Prone
- Best position for accuracy
- Takes time to set up
- Low angle may limit the view

<u>Whenever possible</u>, use a rest to steady your shot.

Shooting Sticks

Bipod

Practice shooting from a variety of positions. Roving games in an area safe to shoot can enhance your shooting ability.

Rifle Sights

Open Sights

REAR SIGHT

FRONT SIGHT

PROPER SIGHT ALIGNMENT

PROPER SIGHT PICTURE

Bullet Impacts

Sighting

PROPER SIGHT ALIGNMENT AND PICTURE

SIGHTS ALIGNED BUT OFF TARGET

SIGHTS OUT OF ALIGNMENT

SIGHTS OUT OF ALIGNMENT AND OFF TARGET

Move rear sight in the direction you want to move the bullet's point of impact

Telescopic Sight

Proper alignment & sight picture.

Common Reticles

Crosshairs with dot

Crosshairs

Post & crosshair

Plex (4 plex shown here)

Selecting a Shotgun

Recoil:
The larger the gauge or the heavier the load, the greater the recoil

Break-action and pump shotguns transfer more energy back through the stock and "kick" harder than semi-automatics.

Common Shotgun Gauges

(Not to Scale)

O
.410 ga.
.410"

O
28 ga.
.530"

O
20 ga.
.615"

O
16 ga.
.670"

O
12 ga.
.729"

O
10 ga.
.775"

Common Chokes

Chokes don't make the shot go farther, they keep the shot together longer to increase the effective range

Full Choke -
Target between 45 and 55 yds

Modified Choke -
Target between 25 and 45 yds

Improved Cylinder -
Target between 15 and 35 yds

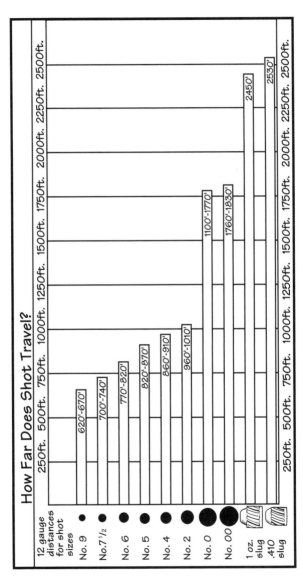

How Far Does Shot Travel?

12 gauge distances for shot sizes		250ft.	500ft.	750ft.	1000ft.	1250ft.	1500ft.	1750ft.	2000ft.	2250ft.	2500ft.
No. 9	●	620'-670'									
No.7¹/₂	●	700'-740'									
No. 6	●	770'-820'									
No. 5	●	820'-870'									
No. 4	●	860'-910'									
No. 2	●	960'-1010'									
No. 0	●	1100'-1770'									
No. 00	●	1760'-1830'									
1 oz. slug		2450'									
.410 slug		2530'									

Recommended Shot for Game

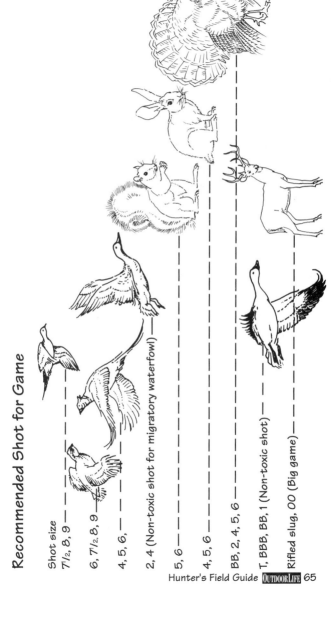

Shot size

7½, 8, 9 ---

6, 7½, 8, 9 ---

4, 5, 6, ---

2, 4 (Non-toxic shot for migratory waterfowl) ---

5, 6 ---

4, 5, 6 ---

BB, 2, 4, 5, 6 ---

T, BBB, BB, 1 (Non-toxic shot) ---

Rifled slug, OO (Big game) ---

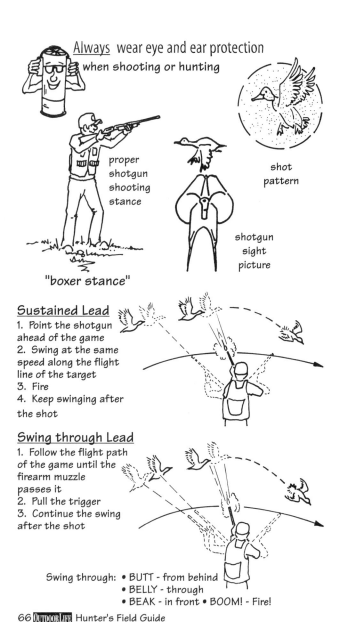

Always wear eye and ear protection when shooting or hunting

proper
shotgun
shooting
stance

shot
pattern

shotgun
sight
picture

"boxer stance"

Sustained Lead
1. Point the shotgun ahead of the game
2. Swing at the same speed along the flight line of the target
3. Fire
4. Keep swinging after the shot

Swing through Lead
1. Follow the flight path of the game until the firearm muzzle passes it
2. Pull the trigger
3. Continue the swing after the shot

Swing through: • BUTT - from behind
• BELLY - through
• BEAK - in front • BOOM! - Fire!

Vital Areas

Areas to place the shot on some typical large & small game

Modern Handgun Actions

Break

- Each shot is loaded by hand
- The spent case is ejected by breaking the action open
- It is loaded only when ready to be fired
- The half-cock position may be unreliable

Revolver

- Rotating cylinders hold cartridges ready to fire
- The cylinder is both magazine & chamber
- The rotating cylinder aligns each cartridge with the barrel
- Modern revolvers are either single action or double action

Semi-automatic

- Is similar to shotgun and rifle actions
- Most have a detachable magazine
- Cartridges are pressed into the magazine
    The magazine is pushed into the bottom of the grip frame
- Semi-automatics feature an action which ejects the spent round, & chambers the next one
- Many semi-automatics have an internal hammer
- Some have a "thumb" or "grip" safety

Bolt

- Is similar to rifle actions
- Each round is loaded by hand
- Spent case is ejected by pulling bolt back

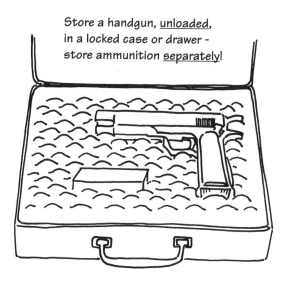

Store a handgun, <u>unloaded</u>, in a locked case or drawer - store ammunition <u>separately</u>!

Handgun shooter's stance and grip

grip as seen from overhead

Whether standing or kneeling, using both hands steadies aim

Shooting & Hunting Games

In addition to getting out on the range, hunters should take advantage of several "games" to improve a variety of shooting skills.

Trap, skeet, & "sporting clays" allow shotgun shooters a chance to shoot at a variety of angles, simulating a variety of game birds & animals.

<u>Silhouette</u> offers the rifle and pistol shooters a chance to shoot at "life-size" targets from a variety of positions & distances.

Visit your local shooting range with your family & enjoy the shooting sports.

Cleaning and Maintenance

Before cleaning any firearm, <u>check</u> <u>to</u> <u>be</u> <u>sure</u> it is unloaded!

For hunting purposes, there is no reason to have a loaded gun in the house. Clean 'em up, then lock 'em up.

<u>Separate</u> and <u>Safe</u>
<u>Guns</u> and <u>Ammo</u>!

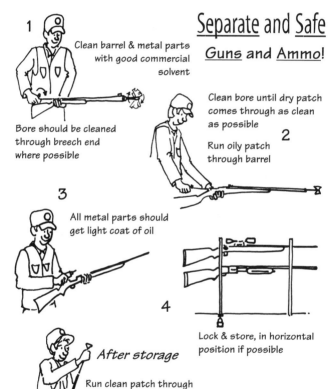

1 Clean barrel & metal parts with good commercial solvent

Bore should be cleaned through breech end where possible

Clean bore until dry patch comes through as clean as possible

2 Run oily patch through barrel

3 All metal parts should get light coat of oil

4 Lock & store, in horizontal position if possible

After storage

Run clean patch through bore before firing

Remove all excess grease & oil before storing, or shooting, firearm

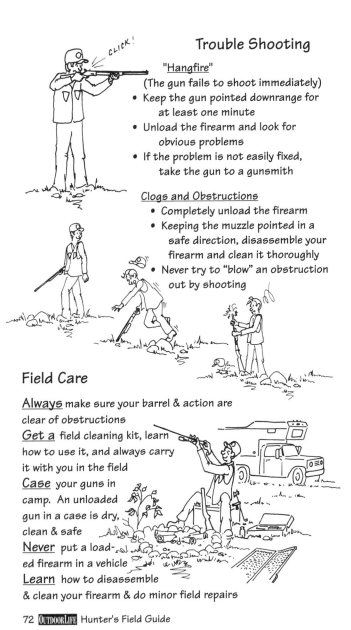

Trouble Shooting

"Hangfire"
(The gun fails to shoot immediately)
- Keep the gun pointed downrange for at least one minute
- Unload the firearm and look for obvious problems
- If the problem is not easily fixed, take the gun to a gunsmith

Clogs and Obstructions
- Completely unload the firearm
- Keeping the muzzle pointed in a safe direction, disassemble your firearm and clean it thoroughly
- Never try to "blow" an obstruction out by shooting

Field Care

<u>Always</u> make sure your barrel & action are clear of obstructions

<u>Get a</u> field cleaning kit, learn how to use it, and always carry it with you in the field

<u>Case</u> your guns in camp. An unloaded gun in a case is dry, clean & safe

<u>Never</u> put a loaded firearm in a vehicle

<u>Learn</u> how to disassemble & clean your firearm & do minor field repairs

OUTDOORLIFE

Shooting Editor Jim Carmichel on:

The Outdoor Life
One-Shot
Sight-In Method

The Outdoor Life one-shot scope sighting-in technique is as easy as 1-2-3; there are only three steps and there is no need for measuring or figuring out how many clicks of the scope's adjustments are needed to make the bullets hit where you aim.

As with any sight-in method, you need a solid support such as a benchrest and sandbags on which to rest the rifle so your aim will be steady. Inexpensive sandbags can be made by cutting the legs of old jeans into 15-inch lengths, tying or sewing the open ends and filling them with sand. You'll need two bags under the forend and one under the butt to make it perfectly steady when you aim your rifle and make the "one-shot" adjustments.

Step 1

With the target set at a distance of 50 to 100 yards, take careful aim, fire one shot and open the action. If the bullet hole cannot be seen through your scope, walk to the target and mark the hole with a paster or felt pen so you will be able to see it clearly. This is important.

Step 2

Aim carefully at the target again, and, without disturbing the rifle and continuing to look at the target through the scope, turn the windage adjustment in the indicated direction. For example, if the shot hit to the right of the bull's eye you will turn

the windage adjustment in the "L" or left direction. It may be easier to have a partner turn the adjustments while you aim and hold the rifle motionless. As the adjustment knob is being turned you will actually see the vertical crosswire march to the bullet hole and when it gets there stop.

Step 3
Now repeat Step 2 with the elevation adjustment until the horizontal crosswire also intersects the bullet hole. What you have done is simply align the crosshairs with your rifle's point of bullet impact, and it will be perfectly—or very nearly—sighted-in. If you accidentally move the rifle during steps 2 or 3 it will be necessary to start again with another shot. It is a good idea to follow up with additional shots to confirm that your rifle is hitting where you aim.

One Shot Sight-In Method

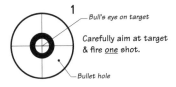

1
Bull's eye on target

Carefully aim at target & fire <u>one</u> shot.

Bullet hole

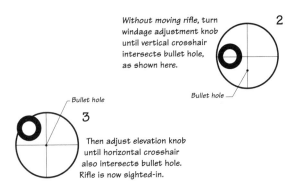

Without moving rifle, turn windage adjustment knob until vertical crosshair intersects bullet hole, as shown here.

2

Bullet hole

Bullet hole

3

Then adjust elevation knob until horizontal crosshair also intersects bullet hole. Rifle is now sighted-in.

Hunting Responsibilities

Putting It All Together

- Consider all of your responsibilities
- Know the area you are going to hunt
- Plan your hunt
- Be prepared and know your limitations
- Develop a good relationship with landowners and managers
- Never use unsafe methods or tactics to approach or attract wildlife
- Never use tactics or methods that place wildlife at an unfair disadvantage
- Clearly identify your target and what lies in front of it and beyond it before you shoot
- Properly care for the meat of the animal
- Respectfully transport the animal home

Be Safe!
Be Legal!
Don't Be a Slob or a Poacher!
Be Ethical!

Responsibilities to Consider—

To Oneself:
- Never lose self-control
- Always be careful, capable and courteous
- Know what to do in an emergency

To Other Hunters:
- Never be rude or hog shots
- Never drink alcohol or use drugs before or while hunting
- Always offer to share the work and any game meat taken

To Non-hunters:
- Never display dead game in or on vehicles when traveling
- Always be courteous and be aware of how your image might affect non-hunters

To Landowners:
- Always secure permission
- Always take care of landowner's property and equipment
- Always be considerate

To the Resource:
- Always learn as much as possible about wildlife
- Always take care of private and public lands
- Always practice or work with conservation efforts
- Understand and obey the hunting laws
- Report hunting violators

Finding Places to Hunt (Checklist)

☐ Identify habitat needs of the game animal you would like to hunt

☐ Find key habitat areas for time of year you plan to hunt

☐ Find out how to gain access

☐ Ask permission or pay appropriate lease fees

☐ Develop a mutually beneficial relationship with landowners or managers of the area you plan to hunt

☐ Be sure of your hunt area, and stay within legal boundaries and areas you have permission to hunt

☐ Scout the hunt area as near as possible to your actual hunt dates

Consult friends, state agencies, managers, chambers of commerce and other sources for more information

Lands

Ask:	Public or	Private ?
☐ <u>Who's in Charge?</u>	Federal, state or county land managers	Private landowners or managers
☐ <u>Is Permission Needed?</u>	Generally open, permits may be required Camping and other access fees may be charged	Verbal or written permission, hunting lease agreement Day, season or yearly lease fees may be charged
☐ <u>Any Restrictions?</u>	Federal and state hunting laws and local ordinances	Federal and state hunting laws <u>and</u> landowner's restrictions
☐ <u>Responsibilities?</u>	Follow rules of safety, and be responsible when camping Clean up after yourself and others Never shoot in camp or in crowded areas Respect the land, hunters and other recreationists	Let the landowner know when you are coming and going and where Don't shoot around buildings, livestock or equipment Clean up after yourself and others Leave gates as you found them, unless told otherwise Fix broken items or let landowner know

Pre-Scouting – Planning the Hunt

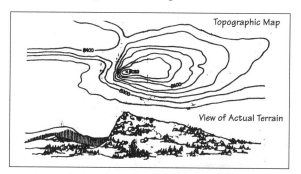

Topographic Map

View of Actual Terrain

Topographic maps use lines to show the contours of the landscape. The closer the lines, the steeper the slope

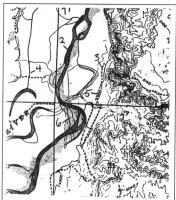

<u>How</u> <u>to</u> <u>Read</u> a Topographic Map:

1. Unless otherwise indicated, the top of the map is north
2. Standing or flowing water (such as the river) is indicated by shaded areas of variable width and shape. Dashed blue lines indicate an intermittent or seasonal water
3. Dashed parallel lines indicate a gravel or graded road, sometimes called an improved road
4. Solid black lines indicate a paved or oiled road
5. Numbers interrupting the contour lines show elevation. Increasing numbers indicate uphill, decreasing numbers, downhill
6. Loosely grouped dotted areas show marsh or wetland areas
7. Single dashed lines show trails

Maps show-
- Roads, trails and access to your hunting area
- Sources of potential water, food or cover
   for wildlife
- Barriers to cross while hunting
- Barriers for wildlife (that can be used to
   your advantage)
- Terrain in which to prepare
- Elevations in which to prepare
- Potential campsites
- Likely travel routes for wildlife

Use a topo map of your area
to make a diagram similar
to this one.

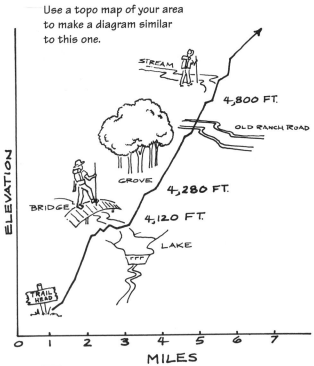

STREAM

4,800 FT.

OLD RANCH ROAD

GROVE

4,280 FT.

BRIDGE

4,120 FT.

LAKE

TRAIL HEAD

ELEVATION

0   1   2   3   4   5   6   7

MILES

Filing A Trip Plan

The Three W's

Where you are going
- Draw a map
- Be specific
- Notify if plans change

Who you are with
- List names
- List contacts
- Give descriptions/photos

When you are returning
- Be specific
- Allow for delays (but not too much time)
- Set "alarm" times

File your trip plan with someone at home and someone in the area you are hunting. List emergency contacts in both areas.

Big-Game Hunter's Kit

Cleaning kit for your gun in the field

Small bag of tools to field strip & repair your gun

Orange vest & hat

Sight-in target to ensure that your gun is performing properly, just before you hunt

Orange surveyor's tape to mark the trail in game recovery, mark the place where you have field-dressed animal - Be sure to retrace the trail & collect tape used to mark the trail

Field-Dressing Kit

Cord for hanging or securing the animal

Knife

Latex gloves

Sharpening stone

Hand towel for cleaning hands & wiping off animal

Game bag

Container for water

Bone saw

Other Necessities

Eye protection

Ear protection

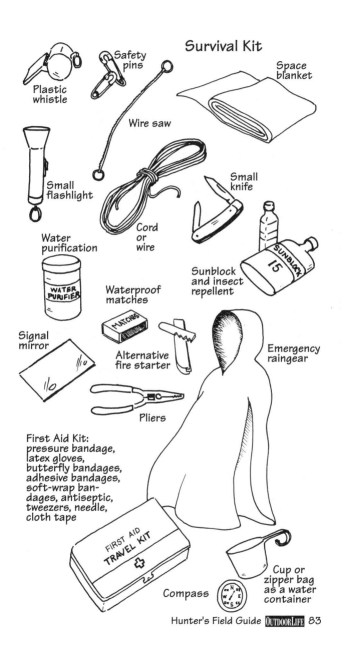

Survival Kit

Plastic whistle

Safety pins

Wire saw

Space blanket

Small flashlight

Cord or wire

Small knife

Water purification

Waterproof matches

Sunblock and insect repellent

Signal mirror

Alternative fire starter

Emergency raingear

Pliers

First Aid Kit: pressure bandage, latex gloves, butterfly bandages, adhesive bandages, soft-wrap bandages, antiseptic, tweezers, needle, cloth tape

FIRST AID TRAVEL KIT

Compass

Cup or zipper bag as a water container

You know you're ready to hunt when...

You are alert, confident and have a safe, ethical attitude

You have your field glasses ready to help you find game and clearly identify your target before you shoot

You've got food to last a couple of days (backpack)

You have your game field care kit with you

You know your hunt area and you've got your map handy

You have your emergency survival and first aid kits handy

You apply waterproof sealer to boots, if you are hunting in snow or a muddy, wet environment

You're always carrying your firearm in a safe and responsible manner

You have clothing appropriate to the area and conditions

You're carrying plenty of water

You have your extra ammo secured in a safe, easy to reach place

You are physically fit, having strength, endurance and flexibility

You've got sturdy boots or shoes that protect your feet and support your ankles

Scouting Tips

* Handshake and a smile:

- Get to know the people in your hunt area
- Ask questions about wildlife, weather, terrain and access
- Note the human patterns. When does the school bus stop on the highway near your hunt area? When does the rancher drive out to check his livestock?
- Make at least one local contact you can reach just prior to your hunt, to find out about current conditions

* Patterns of wildlife use:

- Conduct your scouting just like you would a hunt
- Watch the wildlife, note where the animals go, and when they go there
- Look for sign: tracks, trails, dusting and wallow areas, rubs and scrapes
- Note well-used travel routes, game trails, feeding and watering areas
- Watch other wildlife that use your hunt area. Other animals may give you clues to where hunted animals are located

* Putting it together:

By the time you finish scouting, your field notes should have:
- Hunting routes on a map
- A list of contacts
- Camping spots and rest sites
- Strategies for hunting the area at different times of the day
- Notes on key habitat areas
- Equipment and gear lists to fit the area and conditions

Going Afield

Things to include in a field plan:
- Routes of all hunters marked on a map
- Areas where animals are most likely to be found
- Location for meeting or regrouping
- Schedule for parting and meeting up
- Agreed-upon emergency signals

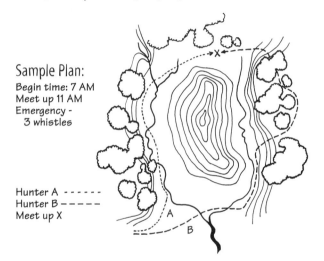

Sample Plan:
Begin time: 7 AM
Meet up 11 AM
Emergency -
   3 whistles

Hunter A - - - - - -
Hunter B - - - - -
Meet up X

"Plan the Hunt —
Hunt the Plan"

Just in Case:

Leave a copy of a map, with your field plan clearly marked, on the driver's seat of your vehicle with:
- Your departure and return times
- Who to contact in case of emergency
- A brief description of all the hunters, their full names and nicknames

A few <u>safe</u> hunting tips:

<u>Don't</u> take an over-the-hill shot.

Two hunters <u>should not</u> shoot at the same game.

When crossing obstacles, open the action and <u>unload</u> - rest muzzle on hat

<u>Don't</u> carry a loaded firearm in a vehicle.

Point firearm in a <u>safe direction</u> when loading, or unloading

Field Carries

Shoulder - used when others are in front or to the side of you

When climbing - always underline unload first

Two-hand - used when others are in front or behind you. Also can be used in the opposite direction of someone to the side of you, but never with others on both sides of you

Sling - used when hiking to and from your main hunting area

Trail - used when others are behind or to the side of you

Cradle - used when others are in front or behind you. Also can be used in the opposite direction if someone is to the side of you, but never with others on both sides of you

Always use a haul line when lifting rifle to a tree, tripod or tower stand - gun unloaded

Elbow - used when others are behind or to the side of you

Zones of Fire

Start with thumbs out to side -
focus on point on far wall - draw arms
staight in until both thumbs are in focus
without moving eyes (about 45°)

This exercise shows
why you only use about
45° when setting zones
of fire

<u>Watch</u> Where You Shoot !

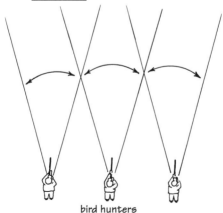

bird hunters
Safe zones of fire

Always <u>POINT</u> <u>MUZZLE</u> <u>AWAY</u>

from yourself

& others!

As hunters move along the trail their relative
position changes and so do <u>safe</u> <u>zones</u> of fire

Field-Dressing Big Game

Make sure game is properly tagged according to state laws before you begin field-dressing

1

- Secure animal on its back by using two large rocks or logs under shoulders & under hips

2

- Using a sharp lock blade or sheath knife, carefully remove sex organs of male animals - <u>Note</u>: In some states or provinces these must stay attached as evidence of sex - Check local game laws

3

- Starting between hind legs, cut down to pelvis and around anus - then turn knife blade up & cut to breast bone as shown, being careful not to puncture intestines or stomach

- Tie intestine vent closed, reach in & cut through windpipe as far up inside neck as possible -cut anything else holding entrails such as the diaphragm muscle

4

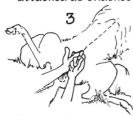

5

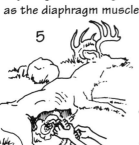

- Lay knife down, roll animal to one side, grasp windpipe with both hands, & pull hard, stripping entrails from body cavity

Field <u>Care</u> of <u>Game</u>

Big Game

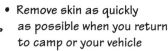

- Remove skin as quickly as possible when you return to camp or your vehicle

- Get the carcass into a gamebag to help it cool and keep flies and dirt off

- Hang the bagged carcass in the shade to cool

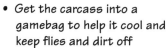

- Do not wrap the carcass or head in plastic at any time

- Keep meat and cape out of the sun, away from the heat

- Allow air to circulate around the meat and cape at all times, even while transporting

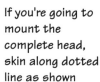

If you're going to mount the complete head, skin along dotted line as shown

Small Game

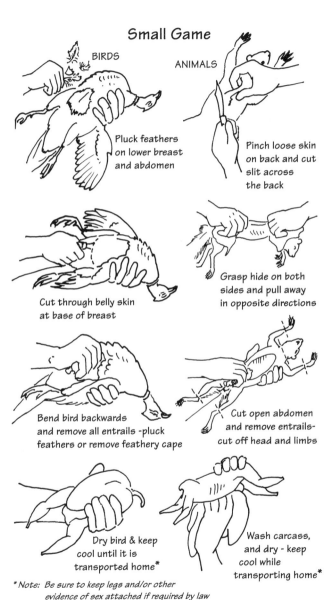

BIRDS

ANIMALS

Pluck feathers on lower breast and abdomen

Pinch loose skin on back and cut slit across the back

Cut through belly skin at base of breast

Grasp hide on both sides and pull away in opposite directions

Bend bird backwards and remove all entrails -pluck feathers or remove feathery cape

Cut open abdomen and remove entrails- cut off head and limbs

Dry bird & keep cool until it is transported home*

Wash carcass, and dry - keep cool while transporting home*

* Note: Be sure to keep legs and/or other evidence of sex attached if required by law

First, make sure your animal is *properly tagged* & is legally yours - (check local regulations)

Transporting Big Game

ATV (back to camp) <u>not</u> on highway

Branches can be tied together to construct a platform for dragging big game

HUNTER ORANGE

Transporting on horseback is desirable in remote areas

If you must carry on shoulders, make sure plenty of Hunter orange is showing

HUNTER ORANGE

Place field-dressed & wrapped animal in vehicle for transporting home or to a cold storage

Be discreet and respectful of the animal as you transport it home. Never make the carcass and head the subject of public display.

OUTDOORLIFE

Shooting Editor Jim Zumbo on:

Five Tips on Hunting From Tree Stands

- Before each hunt, inspect your tree stand for safety. Carefully check the fastening system that secures the stand to the tree, as weather can cause it to deteriorate or shift about. Be sure your climbing spikes are sound and capable of supporting your weight. Make sure you have a string or rope attached to the stand (or within reaching distance) to pull your bow or unloaded firearm up when you're comfortably in place. Always wear a safety belt or harness that secures you to the tree.

- Locate your stand between feeding and bedding areas. Scout your area before hunting season and find places where deer actively feed. They typically use trails to walk from feeding spots to bedding locations in the forest. Some trails are primary ones, being used much more extensively than secondary trails. The amount of wear and tracks on a trail should be a clue to its degree of use. Put your stand as far from the trail as you can, keeping it well within the shooting-range limits of your bow or firearm. Check the prevailing wind direction and always place your stand downwind of the trail.

- In some areas it's difficult to locate active feeding areas, which makes it hard to place your stand in a good spot. If the rut is on, look for scrapes and rubs, which indicate areas of whitetail deer activity. Bucks commonly visit these sites on a daily basis, especially just prior to and during the peak of the rut. Seek fresh scrapes. If you find several of them along an old road or edge of cover, place your stand where the scrapes are in sight. Be prepared for a buck to come in any time of the day.

- During the day you should remain in your stand as long as possible if other hunters are about. They will keep deer moving. Be especially vigilant during the midday hours from 10 a.m. to 2 p.m., since that's when most hunters are heading in and out of the woods for lunch. A midday stand often works best in a spot where adjacent woodlots come together to form a natural funnel. Most deer travel in these funnels to avoid openings.

- In dry areas, deer will drink water every day, especially late in the afternoon before they come out to feed, or in the morning before they head to bedding areas. Before setting up a stand near a water source, check the area for fresh tracks to determine whether deer are using the area. The most promising waterholes are those that are far apart. Too many water sources will allow deer to choose from a greater selection of watering areas, decreasing your chances of seeing your quarry. Deer often seem to be very alert at watering areas, so be extra careful to avoid moving and making noise.

Outdoor Skills

<u>Your</u> Responsibilities:

- Be physically & mentally fit before heading outdoors

- Be courteous on the trail, in camp, & in the field

- Take care of the land, public or private

- Respect landowners & land managers at all times

- Be prepared for any terrain or conditions

- Always set up a camp that is safe, efficient & low impact

- Know how to safely use & maintain your equipment

- Avoid dangerous & threatening situations

- Know first-aid & survival techniques

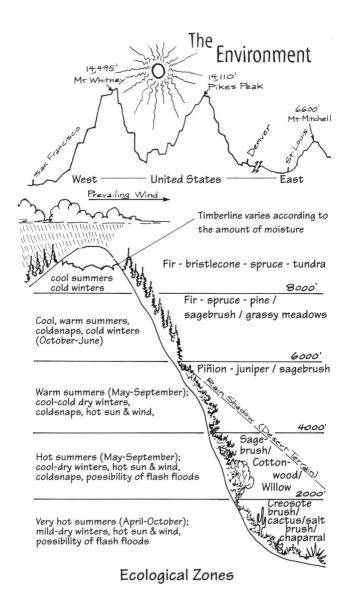

The Environment

14,495'
Mt. Whitney

14,110'
Pikes Peak

6600'
Mt. Mitchell

San Francisco

Denver

St. Louis

West —— United States —— East

Prevailing Wind

Timberline varies according to the amount of moisture

Fir - bristlecone - spruce - tundra

cool summers
cold winters

8000'

Fir - spruce - pine /
sagebrush / grassy meadows

Cool, warm summers,
coldsnaps, cold winters
(October-June)

6000'

Piñion - juniper / sagebrush

Warm summers (May-September);
cool-cold dry winters,
coldsnaps, hot sun & wind,

Rain Shadow (Desert Terrain)

4000'

Sage-
brush/
Cotton-
wood/
Willow

Hot summers (May-September);
cool-dry winters, hot sun & wind,
coldsnaps, possibility of flash floods

2000'

Creosote
brush/
cactus/salt
brush/
chaparral

Very hot summers (April-October);
mild-dry winters, hot sun & wind,
possibility of flash floods

Ecological Zones

Preparations

Spring
<u>Clothing</u>: Layered, sweater or jacket, cap, medium gloves, long-sleeved shirt & wool pants, sturdy hiking boots, heavy socks

<u>Food</u>: High carbohydrates & fats, nuts, jerky, meats, starches, bread & water

<u>Equipment</u>: For fire building, for shelter, knife & ax, car tools, for field care of game, for cooking, flashlight

Summer
Essentially the same except for lightweight clothing & boots, and the addition of hat, sunscreen, fruits, vegetables, and <u>lots</u> <u>of</u> <u>water</u>

Fall
<u>Clothing</u>: Layered, sweater or jacket, cap, medium gloves, long-sleeved shirt & wool pants, sturdy hiking boots, heavy socks

<u>Food</u>: High carbohydrates & fats, nuts, jerky, meats, starches, bread & water

<u>Equipment</u>: For fire building, for shelter, knife & ax, car tools, flashlight, tools for field care of game, for cooking

Winter
Essentially the same except for heavier clothing layers & underwear, heavy waterproof/windproof coat, insulated boots, & tire chains

TYPE OF COUNTRY

Dry, rocky, forest, open

Rainy, forest, open

Swamp, marsh

Reading the Clouds & Weather Patterns

Clouds

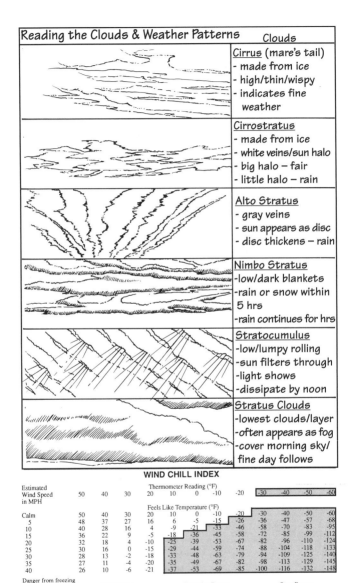

Cirrus (mare's tail)
- made from ice
- high/thin/wispy
- indicates fine weather

Cirrostratus
- made from ice
- white veins/sun halo
- big halo — fair
- little halo — rain

Alto Stratus
- gray veins
- sun appears as disc
- disc thickens — rain

Nimbo Stratus
- low/dark blankets
- rain or snow within 5 hrs
- rain continues for hrs

Stratocumulus
- low/lumpy rolling
- sun filters through
- light shows
- dissipate by noon

Stratus Clouds
- lowest clouds/layer
- often appears as fog
- cover morning sky/ fine day follows

WIND CHILL INDEX

Estimated Wind Speed in MPH	Thermometer Reading (°F)											
	50	40	30	20	10	0	-10	-20	-30	-40	-50	-60
	Feels Like Temperature (°F)											
Calm	50	40	30	20	10	0	-10	-20	-30	-40	-50	-60
5	48	37	27	16	6	-5	-15	-26	-36	-47	-57	-68
10	40	28	16	4	-9	-21	-33	-46	-58	-70	-83	-95
15	36	22	9	-5	-18	-36	-45	-58	-72	-85	-99	-112
20	32	18	4	-10	-25	-39	-53	-67	-82	-96	-110	-124
25	30	16	0	-15	-29	-44	-59	-74	-88	-104	-118	-133
30	28	13	-2	-18	-33	-48	-63	-79	-94	-109	-125	-140
35	27	11	-4	-20	-35	-49	-67	-82	-98	-113	-129	-145
40	26	10	-6	-21	-37	-53	-69	-85	-100	-116	-132	-148

Danger from freezing of exposed flesh (with proper clothing)

Little Danger   Increasing Danger   Great Danger

YOUR BODY LOSES HEAT _25 TIMES FASTER_ WHEN IT IS WET !

Exposure Forces at Work
(Hot moves to cold)

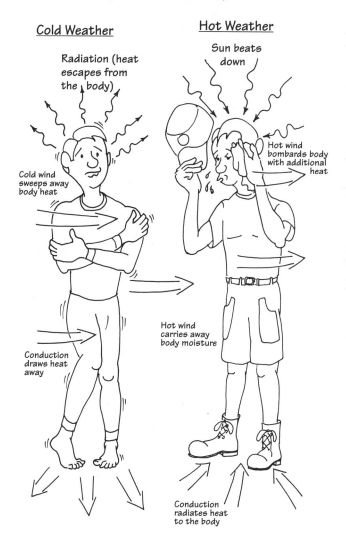

Clothing

Having the proper clothing can make the difference between a safe, enjoyable hunt and misery—or even death.

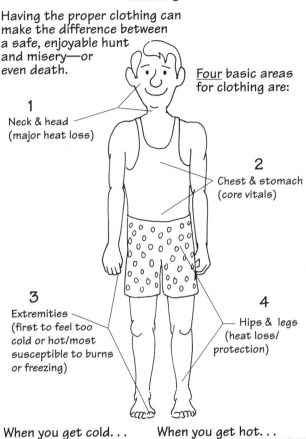

1
Neck & head (major heat loss)

<u>Four</u> basic areas for clothing are:

2
Chest & stomach (core vitals)

3
Extremities (first to feel too cold or hot/most susceptible to burns or freezing)

4
Hips & legs (heat loss/ protection)

When you get cold. . .	When you get hot. . .
Heat escapes	Body overheats
Blood pulled into core vitals	Body perspires to cool off
Extremities left with less blood	Body dehydrates
Extremities freeze/core cools	Fever can develop
<u>Hypothermia/frostbite</u>	<u>Heat</u> <u>exhaustion</u>/
can result !	<u>heat</u> <u>stroke</u> can result !

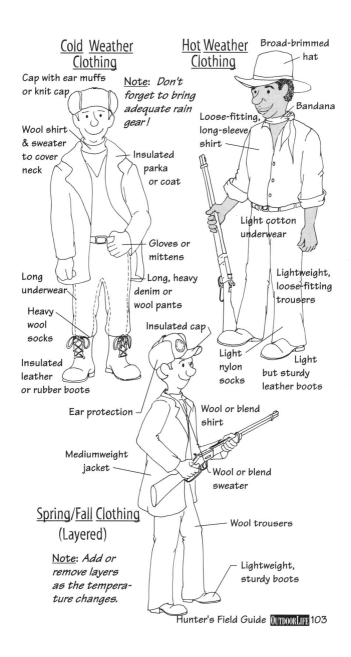

Cold Weather Clothing

Cap with ear muffs or knit cap

Note: *Don't forget to bring adequate rain gear!*

Wool shirt & sweater to cover neck

Insulated parka or coat

Long underwear

Gloves or mittens

Long, heavy denim or wool pants

Heavy wool socks

Insulated leather or rubber boots

Hot Weather Clothing

Broad-brimmed hat

Bandana

Loose-fitting, long-sleeve shirt

Light cotton underwear

Lightweight, loose-fitting trousers

Light nylon socks

Light but sturdy leather boots

Insulated cap

Ear protection

Wool or blend shirt

Mediumweight jacket

Wool or blend sweater

Wool trousers

Lightweight, sturdy boots

Spring/Fall Clothing
(Layered)

Note: *Add or remove layers as the temperature changes.*

Hunter's Field Guide **OUTDOOR LIFE** 103

Camp Tools

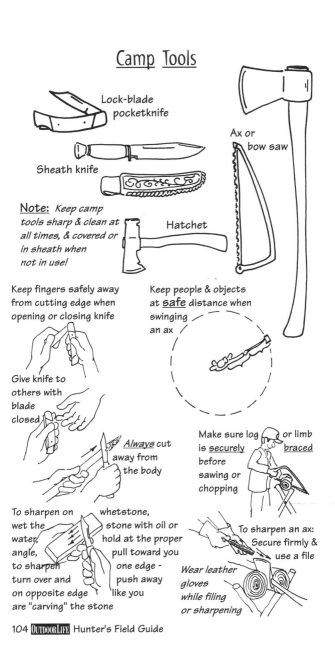

Lock-blade pocketknife

Sheath knife

Ax or bow saw

Note: *Keep camp tools sharp & clean at all times, & covered or in sheath when not in use!*

Hatchet

Keep fingers safely away from cutting edge when opening or closing knife

Keep people & objects at **safe** distance when swinging an ax

Give knife to others with blade closed

Always cut away from the body

Make sure log or limb is <u>securely</u> <u>braced</u> before sawing or chopping

To sharpen on whetstone, wet the water, stone with oil or hold at the proper angle, to sharpen pull toward you turn over and one edge - on opposite edge push away are "carving" the stone like you

To sharpen an ax: Secure firmly & use a file

Wear leather gloves while filing or sharpening

How to Use Woods Tools

Note: Be sure to follow all wood-cutting rules, especially on public lands.

1. Use bow saw to cut down small dead trees or cut off larger dead branches.

2. Trim limbs from downed dead trees with a hand ax or larger ax. Stand on opposite side of limb or trunk.

3. Cut tree trunk into firewood length with a bow saw.

4. Cut up smaller branches with hand ax, using contact method and cutting at an angle.

5. Split large pieces of firewood with an ax by placing them against a chopping log. Keep hands low and feet separated behind the chopping log.

6. Use contact method to split wood into kindling.

7. Make fuzz sticks from kindling to speed up fire starting.

8. To carry an ax, hold handle next to head with bit facing out and down. Carry hand ax with hand around head, handle down, and bit to rear.

9. Learn to pass an ax safely: Hold handle near knob with head down, and pass to other person with bit facing out at right angles between you. Then take firm grip on handle just below your hand.

10. Keep woods tools covered or sheathed when they are not in use. Axes can be stuck in log with handle running up the log. Saws should be covered with cloth or an old piece of garden hose.

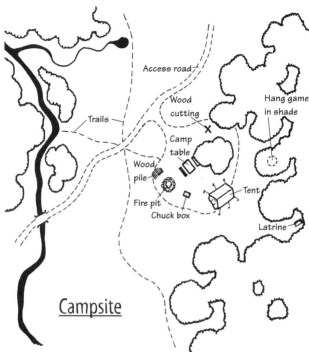

Campsite

- Use established campsite if possible
- Find a place with easy access to a roadway
- Find a place to hang game animals in cool shade
- Avoid camping too near water to avoid pollution
- Never litter & keep trampling to a minimum
- Make sure any fire is <u>cold-out</u> before leaving
- Pack out all trash & accessories

Complete your campsite by preparing for waste disposal— *Dig your latrines at least 75 steps from camps, trails, or water sources & bury them before you leave*

Building an Open Fire

- Collect wood as the camp is set up
- Do all wood collection while it is still light
- Collect enough at one time to avoid running out
- Consider all fire needs when building wood site
- Place two poles parallel on ground and stack firewood on poles to protect it from dampness
- Stack wood at least 10 feet from fire
- Cover with a tarp or plastic poncho

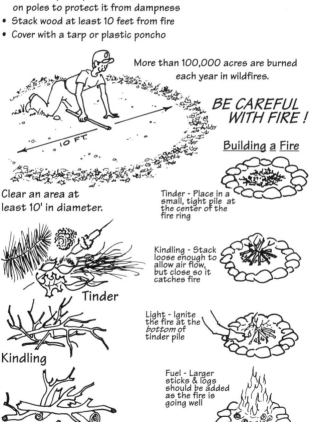

More than 100,000 acres are burned each year in wildfires.

BE CAREFUL WITH FIRE !

Clear an area at least 10' in diameter.

10 FT.

Building a Fire

Tinder - Place in a small, tight pile at the center of the fire ring

Kindling - Stack loose enough to allow air flow, but close so it catches fire

Light - Ignite the fire at the *bottom* of tinder pile

Fuel - Larger sticks & logs should be added as the fire is going well

Tinder

Kindling

Fuel

Food Preparation

It is more difficult to refrigerate food outdoors -
Take special care with meats and milks -
Get more ice than you'll need

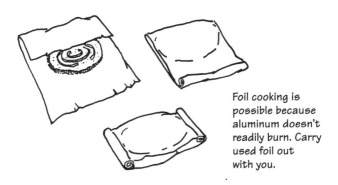

Foil cooking is
possible because
aluminum doesn't
readily burn. Carry
used foil out
with you.

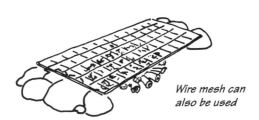

*Wire mesh can
also be used*

If no wire mesh is
available, rest a
long stick on a
forked support so
that it can hold
food over the fire.
Wrap food around
the stick.

Cooking With a Tin

Stand the tin on some rocks so that a fire can be lit beneath it. Build up rocks and earth - or, better, clay - around back and sides and over it, but leaving a space behind for heat and smoke to move around the back.

Use a stick to make a chimney hole from above to the space at the back.

Alternatives to Open Fire

Backpack stove (propane)

Campstove - (white gas)

Shelters

Examples that can be constructed with tarp, rope, & local materials

Lean-to

Hanging fly

Dining fly

Half fly

Pup tent

Anchors

Deadman

Snowfluke

For anchoring shelters in snow

Tents & Bedding

Sleeping bag shapes

Rectangular

Modified Mummy

Mummy

Quilting

Double-offset quilting

Box quilting

Straight quilting

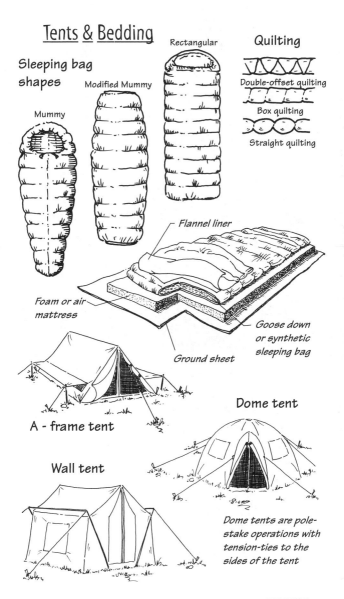

Flannel liner

Foam or air mattress

Goose down or synthetic sleeping bag

Ground sheet

A - frame tent

Dome tent

Wall tent

Dome tents are pole-stake operations with tension-ties to the sides of the tent

Backpacks

Proper pack weight distribution

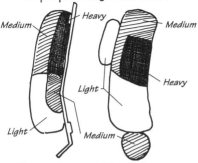

External frame pack   Internal frame pack

Steps a, b, c, & d show how to tie a <u>diamond hitch</u>, one of the most popular with backpackers

Steps 1, 2, & 3 show proper way to lift & shoulder your backpack.

<u>Wilderness</u> <u>Survival</u> <u>Checklist</u>

Carry these in your <u>pockets</u>:

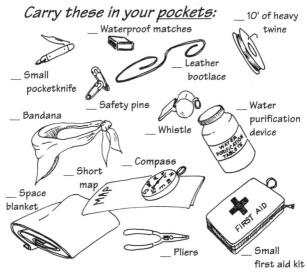

__ Waterproof matches

__ 10' of heavy twine

__ Small pocketknife

__ Leather bootlace

__ Safety pins

__ Bandana

__ Whistle

__ Water purification device

__ Short map

__ Compass

__ Space blanket

__ Pliers

__ Small first aid kit

Carry these in your <u>pack</u>:

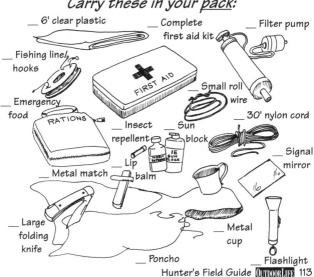

__ 6' clear plastic

__ Complete first aid kit

__ Filter pump

__ Fishing line/ hooks

__ Emergency food

__ Small roll wire

__ 30' nylon cord

__ Insect repellent

__ Sun block

__ Signal mirror

__ Metal match

__ Lip balm

__ Large folding knife

__ Metal cup

__ Poncho

__ Flashlight

Planning & Preparation

It's always easier to set up a tent, the first time, when the sun is shining.

Get ready!

- Know the terrain & conditions
- Assume the worst - be prepared
- Plan for several survival scenarios

Get set!

- Minimize items - maximize use
- Learn outdoor lore
- Study current survival techniques

Go!

- Review condition of emergency gear and how to use it before you go out
- Practice survival techniques
- Camp out with others - camp alone, (under controlled conditions)

<u>Trail</u> <u>Savvy</u>

A little effort can go a long way toward saving the natural beauty of your favorite hunting spot.

Here are a few things you can do:

- Keep picketed horses well away from camp, lakes & streams

- Move picketed horses often

- Tie horses to highline stretched between <u>sturdy</u> trees

- When using horses, take the minimum number of animals needed

- Leave pets at home, or keep them under control at all times

- Leave the landscape <u>*better*</u> than you found it, for others to enjoy

- Stay on the designated trail while hiking or riding

- Avoid cutting across switchbacks

<u>Three</u> <u>Terrific</u> <u>Tips</u>

To keep from getting lost

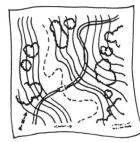

<u>Short</u> <u>map</u>: Carry a "short"map (cut down or reduced to show the area you're traveling), know how to read it & identify features & landmarks on the map before you take off.

<u>Back</u> <u>trail</u>: Stop often to look back down the trail you just traveled. "Backtrail" to get a feeling for what the country looks like from the opposite direction.

<u>Landmarks</u>: Look for odd shapes or features that stand out to remind you of where you have been.
Make sketches & notes, if necessary - keep the landmarks in the correct sequence.

S. T. O. P.

You're Lost!

Stay put!
Moving around :
- Wastes energy
- Makes you anxious
- Makes you harder to find

Admit it !

Think
- What do you remember to help find yourself?
- What do you have with you?
- What is there around you that you can use?
- What should you do to get safe & comfortable?

Organize
- Your stuff
- Your time
- Your activities

Prepare
- For safety and comfort
- For night time
- Weather conditions
- Rescue/signaling
- Your rescue/homecoming party

AIR – minutes

WARMTH – hours

How long can you last without these?!

3

If you are expecting to be rescued within 24 to 78 hours, what is most urgent !

WATER – days

FOOD – weeks

Estimating Travel Time

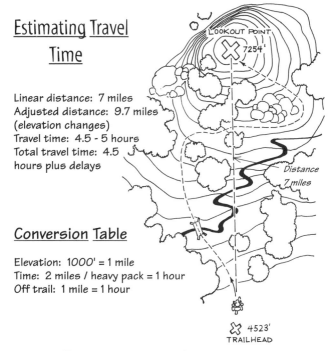

Linear distance: 7 miles
Adjusted distance: 9.7 miles
(elevation changes)
Travel time: 4.5 - 5 hours
Total travel time: 4.5 hours plus delays

Conversion Table

Elevation: 1000' = 1 mile
Time: 2 miles / heavy pack = 1 hour
Off trail: 1 mile = 1 hour

How to Obtain your Bearing from a Map

To travel from your present location to some destination on the map:

1. Place your compass on the map so that the long edge of the base is on a line from your present location to the desired destination.

2. Hold the compass steady, rotate the dial so that the "N" on the dial is pointed True North on the map. Your bearing now appears on the dial at the sighting line.

3. Pick the compass up and hold it in a horizontal position so that the magnetic needle is free to rotate. Pivot yourself until the orienting arrow is aligned with the magnetic needle. The compass now points in the direction you need to travel to reach your desired destination.

How big are the dangers?

Drowning (major cause)

Falls and slides (_**#1 cause**_ of injuries)

Cold Wind (major cause)

Sun & Heat (major cause)

Wildlife (very rare)

Rockfall, Avalanche or Landslides (rare)

Lightning (rare)

Wildfire (extremely rare)

Slides & Falls

Point

Sweep

If hiking in a group:
Place stronger hikers
at point & sweep (rear),
as shown here

*Learn roping techniques for groups,
and zig-zag across mountains as
shown by dashed line above*

Use a walking
stick for
balance &
support

If you slip
or fall - use the
stick as a brake &
spread out to create drag

Avalanches &
Rock Slides

- Always be aware of what's above you
- New snow over old snow is <u>very</u> <u>dangerous</u>
- Avoid steep aspects

One More River to Cross
Safety Around Running Water

- Study the river before crossing - walk along edge & look for best possible place to cross
- Look for the wide, shallow areas, which are usually safest
- Avoid the main current - eddy hop
- If you can't see the bottom, it's probably too deep to wade across
- Watch for debris floating in river
- Look for sand, gravel or cobble bottom
- Look for gradual slopes to enter & exit (avoid cutbanks)

Gauging Depths

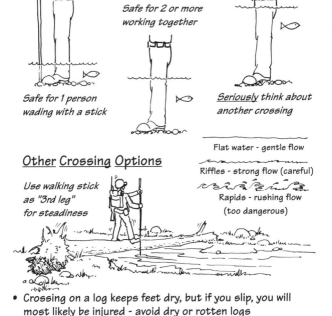

Safe for 2 or more working together

Safe for 1 person wading with a stick

Seriously think about another crossing

Flat water - gentle flow

Riffles - strong flow (careful)

Rapids - rushing flow (too dangerous)

Other Crossing Options

Use walking stick as "3rd leg" for steadiness

- Crossing on a log keeps feet dry, but if you slip, you will most likely be injured - avoid dry or rotten logs
- Rock-hopping - be careful if rocks are slippery or loose
- Run a taut rope to solid anchors on each bank, if possible
- Use a canoe or john boat when possible
- _Do not cross_ if it looks dangerous - walk to safer crossing

<u>Water</u> <u>Safety</u> <u>Procedures</u>

Safely enter canoe or boat

Keep your center of gravity low, & move in slowly, transferring your weight to the bottom center of boat. Reverse maneuver to exit.

If you fall or get swept away . . .

Float on your back, keep your feet up in front of you.
Don't try to stand in fast water.
Use your hands to maneuver until you reach shallower water.
Use your feet to push off obstacles. Falling into cold, deep water can result in *hypothermia.*

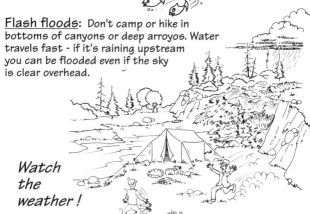

<u>Flash floods</u>: Don't camp or hike in bottoms of canyons or deep arroyos. Water travels fast - if it's raining upstream you can be flooded even if the sky is clear overhead.

Watch the weather !

Shelters

Best: Find a natural shelter

- Rock overhangs
- Crevice or cave
- Tree well in snow
- Deadfalls
- Hollow log

Next best: Find a shelter easily enlarged

Deadfalls or woodpile

Brush or debris pile

Depression or piles in the snow or earth

Least best: A shelter from scratch

<u>Shelter building</u> takes time and energy, and should never be undertaken in extreme heat or cold unless absolutely necessary.

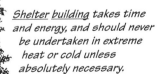

Building <u>Survival</u> <u>Fires</u>

1

Be selective and gather very fine dead twigs from lower limbs of standing trees.

WIND

2

Shelter tinder from rain or snow with your body, and keep your back to the wind.

3

Hold twigs in hand in upright position.

4

Use two or more matches, and hold under twigs.

5

Hold twigs until burning readily, then put on ground igniting tinder pile.

If it starts to rain or snow, take fuel with you into the shelter. *Keep it dry!*

Signaling

Be Visible !

Flares: Can be seen at a distance • but only a few shots available •combustible & could cause fires

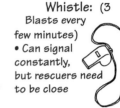

Mirror: Endless resource for signaling - Must have sunlight

Whistle: (3 Blasts every few minutes) • Can signal constantly, but rescuers need to be close

3 Signal Fires: Need to be 10' apart using green, smoky fuel - rain or snow may inhibit fire

Ground Symbols: Use rocks or logs on high, open ground

Gone in this direction

Help

Semaphores

All OK   I Need Help   No   Yes

Hunter's Field Guide **OutdoorLife** 125

Obtaining Water

<u>All</u> water in North America should be considered contaminated. *Organic* contamination is bacteria from animal or vegetable matter. *Mineral* contamination comes from commercial and natural sources.

Purification Methods

Boil at least 10 minutes

Treat with water purifier

Distill as last resort (inefficient)

Use filter

Tie a plastic bag around a leafy branch, or suspend it over a bush. Don't let bag touch the leaves. Water will collect at bottom of bag.

A water "still" can also be constructed as shown. You need a sheet of plastic, a container & a drinking tube. Dig a hole of the approximate dimensions specified. Add vegetation, & douse the ground in hole with impure water. It will evaporate and then condense, filling your container with clean water.

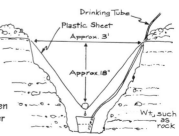

Drinking Tube
Plastic Sheet
Approx. 3'
Approx. 18"
Wt., such as rock

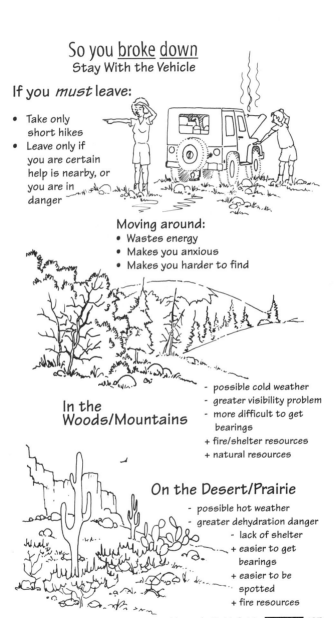

So you <u>broke</u> <u>down</u>
Stay With the Vehicle

If you *must* leave:

- Take only short hikes
- Leave only if you are certain help is nearby, or you are in danger

Moving around:
- Wastes energy
- Makes you anxious
- Makes you harder to find

In the Woods/Mountains

- possible cold weather
- greater visibility problem
- more difficult to get bearings
+ fire/shelter resources
+ natural resources

On the Desert/Prairie

- possible hot weather
- greater dehydration danger
- lack of shelter
+ easier to get bearings
+ easier to be spotted
+ fire resources

Road Sense

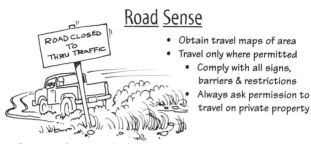

- Obtain travel maps of area
- Travel only where permitted
  - Comply with all signs, barriers & restrictions
  - Always ask permission to travel on private property

- Stay out of streams & off lake shores or marshes where you have the potential to get stuck or mired
- Avoid muddy trails, roads, meadows or steep hillsides where your tires can tear the terrain

- Respect the rights of hikers, riders, campers & others to enjoy their activities
- Slow down & be courteous in camp areas
- When encountering mountain bikers or horses, pull over & stop
- Never chase wildlife or livestock with any type of vehicle

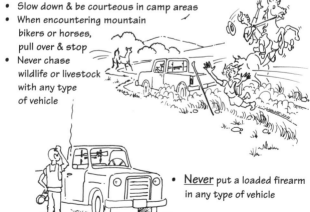

- <u>Never</u> put a loaded firearm in any type of vehicle

Wildlife Savvy

Bear

<u>Precautions</u>: Be especially alert around "dirty" campsites, trash dumps, thick brush, berry patches, & streams/lakes

<u>Triggers</u>: Startled - food - have cubs - are wounded

<u>Prevention</u>: Hunters in bear country should be familiar with potential threats that all bears pose keep a clean camp, hang food & sweet-smelling goods out of reach of camp, make some noise when hiking, never approach young bears, avoid their feeding areas

<u>Encounters</u>: Don't make eye contact, stop, talk quietly, then move slowly. If attacked - Curl up in ball & cover vital areas - (kick, punch & yell as last resort)

<u>Precautions</u>: Be alert around brushy areas, open/grassy or wooded edges

<u>Triggers</u>: Startled - approached - chased - rutting

<u>Prevention</u>: Make noise while traveling thru cover, never approach bison, leave area if bulls seem aggressive

Bison

<u>Encounters</u>: Move away slowly, find cover or leave the area - If attacked, <u>run</u> to nearest cover !

Deer

<u>Precautions</u>: Be alert when approaching a deer that's down, until you're sure it's dead

<u>Triggers</u>: Startled - approached - rutting

<u>Prevention</u>: Make noise while moving thru cover if you're not hunting, stay near cover during rut

<u>Encounters</u>: Stop - deer will run away if given a chance - If attacked, move quickly out of the way & find cover (punch, kick, & yell as last resort)

Moose

Precautions: Be alert around brushy areas, near water, ponds & marshes, rivers/streams

Triggers: Startled - approached or chased - cows with calves

Prevention: If you're not hunting, make noise while walking thru cover. Give moose a wide berth, especially cows with calves.

Encounters: Put cover between you & the moose, Quietly & slowly leave the area - If attacked - <u>run</u> for nearest cover

Mountain Lion

Precautions: Be alert around rocky, brushy areas and steep, wooded areas

Triggers: Running away like prey - cat is hungry - young are nearby - are wounded

Prevention: Try not to run or jog in lion territory, never approach a lion kill, never approach <u>any</u> mountain lion

Encounters: Stop, try not to make eye contact, make yourself look "big," shout - If attacked, curl up & protect vital areas - kick, punch or yell as last resort

Venomous Snakes

Precautions: Be alert around rimrock, rockpiles, woodpiles, grassy areas, deadfall, wooded areas near water

Triggers: Startled - approached or bothered

Prevention: Wear high-topped, leather boots or snake leggings, carry a walking stick & make noise as you tap ground, brush & grass in front of you

Encounters: Stop, allow the snake to escape or walk around it - If bitten, get medical attention immediately

First Aid

Warning, Hunters - this is only a field guide to treat minor injuries or emergencies. It's the hunter's <u>responsibility</u> to attend a

CERTIFIED FIRST-AID & CPR COURSE
(AMERICAN HEART ASSOCIATION OR RED CROSS)

HEAD - TO - TOE EXAMINATION FOR INJURY SHOULD INCLUDE:
Head, neck, shoulders, chest, arms, abdomen, back, pelvis, legs & feet

VITAL SIGNS YOU CAN CHECK:
Level of consciousness, pupils, pulse, skin color, body temperature, respiration & response to stimulus

But First!
The Primary Survey

Establish Responsiveness

Shake & Shout
"Are you all right!"

If there is no response, begin the ABCs of CPR

A Tilt head back & lift chin up with fingers under jaw to establish <u>A</u>irway (Move head as little as possible if there may be a neck injury)

Look, listen & feel for <u>B</u>reathing - Is chest moving? If not, give 2 breaths **B**

Check for <u>C</u>irculation - Is there a pulse? Place two fingers in groove of neck on either side of Adam's apple

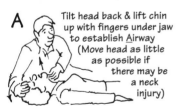

H

Adam's apple

C

Carotid artery

Check for <u>H</u>emorrhaging (bleeding) Is there blood-soaked clothing? Are there pools of blood on ground?

Cardio - Pulmonary - Resuscitation
CPR

First - Tilt head back & lift chin up, pinch victim's nose shut

Blow 2 slow breaths into victim's mouth (2 seconds for adults, 1-1½ for children)
- inhale after each breath
- watch for chest to rise
- allow deflation after each breath
- reposition neck if necessary

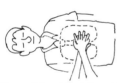

Check pulse - put 2 fingers in groove of neck nearest you - if there is no pulse, begin chest compressions

Slide fingers up rib cage to notch in middle of chest

Put index finger in notch & slide heel of other hand next to fingers

Now put hand that found the rib notch on top of other hand, & press downward with heel of bottom hand about 1½ - 2 inches, making sure to keep your arms straight <u>NOTE</u>: Use only one hand on a child or small or aged adult

Keep this procedure up, alternating breaths & compressions:
- 2 breaths
- 15 compressions (one-and-two-and...)
- 2 breaths - continue until victim breathes or help arrives

Check pulse & breathing regularly for any response

Shock

Hypovolemic Shock (from fluid or blood loss)
What to look for:

- Restlessness, anxiety, weakness
- Pale or blueish skin & lips
  - Moist, clammy skin
  - Thirst
  - Nausea, vomiting
  - Unconsciousness
  - Weak pulse

*Straighten victim's
legs & elevate above
heart 8" to 12"*

What to do:
Seek medical attention ASAP: • Give fluids as tolerated

Choking

What to look for:
- Unable to speak, breathe, or cough
- Clutching neck with one or both hands
- Wheezing, gurgling noise in throat
- Skin turning blue or ashen color

Heimlich Maneuver

*Stand behind victim with arms around
victim's torso. Clench one hand over the
other, thumb side of fist pressing between
the waist & bottom of ribs. Apply
pressure & jerk quickly upwards 4 times.*

*If alone, use your
own fists & arms -
or push down
against any blunt
projection.*

Sometimes objects can be dislodged by a
finger sweep. (Caution: When inserting your
finger in any patient's mouth, be extremely
careful of the risk of being bitten.) Grasp
victim's jaw & tongue & lift upward - use
hooking motion inside mouth from one
cheek to other. (Be sure victim is choking &
not experiencing a seizure.)

Hunter's Field Guide OUTDOORLIFE 133

External Bleeding

Direct pressure stops most bleeding. Place sterile gauze or clean cloth over wound & apply pressure. If bleeding doesn't stop in 5 minutes, replace cloth and continue to apply direct pressure to wound while adding pressure to pressure points (below).

X Denotes spot to apply pressure if
bleeding persists in indicated body areas

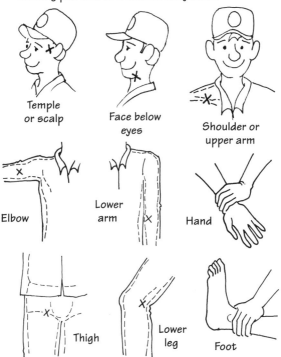

Temple
or scalp

Face below
eyes

Shoulder or
upper arm

Elbow

Lower
arm

Hand

Thigh

Lower
leg

Foot

* _Use a tourniquet only as last resort, & never apply below the elbow or knee_

DO NOT: • Use direct pressure on eye, embedded objects or open fractures
• Rinse wound with full-strength medicines
• Close wounds with tape
• Breathe or blow on a wound

Head Injuries

What to look for:

- Unconsciousness
- Memory loss
- Vomiting or nausea
- Seizures
- Unequal pupils
- Weakness or paralysis
- Combativeness - with victim striking out randomly at nearest person
- Headache, vision impairment, loss of balance
- Blood or clear fluid leaking from ears or nose

Note! The signs & symptoms of brain injury may be observed immediately (as listed above) or may slowly develop over several hours.

<u>Check</u> <u>out</u> the victim by asking personal questions: name, birthday, home address, where they are, etc. If the victim can't answer these questions, it could indicate a concussion, or closed head injury.

Seek medical attention immediately !

Spinal Injury

If victim is sitting up, support their head between your arms & gently lean them backward - making sure you keep their head & neck immobilized - if you must go for help, stabilize the head on both sides with objects

Tell victim not to move!

Note! Spinal injuries can be difficult to evaluate. If you suspect one (pain over neck or spine, inability to move arms or legs, tingling or numbness in arms or legs, inability to wiggle toes or to feel your touch on soles of feet...)

<u>Do</u> <u>not</u> move victim unless it is absolutely necessary for safety reasons (victim is in dangerous place).

In most cases, you should just stabilize the victim & wait for professional help to arrive.

Dislocations & Sprains
What <u>to</u> <u>do</u>

A _dislocation_ is displacement of a bone end from its normal position at the joint

> **<u>Example</u>:** Displacement of humerus (upper arm bone) from shoulder socket

Can cause a deformed-looking shoulder

Prepare a splint with a thin board or foam board & wrap with bandages or clean cloth (T-shirt, etc.)

Arm & shoulder joints can be additionally stabilized by fashioning a _sling & swathe_ as shown here

Seek medical attention as soon as possible !

Splint with boot on

Rest
Ice
Compression
Elevation

If you suspect an ankle sprain, use the RICE procedures listed at left. Do not apply heat until at least 48 hours after the injury - If swelling & pain don't decrease within 48 hours, seek medical attention.

If you are hiking & sprain your ankle - Construct a splint <u>over</u> your boot until you return to camp or vehicle - Once boot is removed, hiking is finished - Don't push an injured ankle!

Fractures — _What to do_

Check: **C**irculation

Sensation

Movement

If body part is bent or deformed, apply gentle traction & apply a splint

You can fold a triangular bandage into a sling

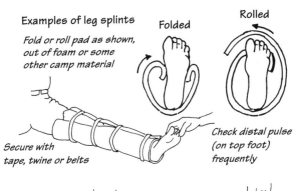

Tie around the back of patient's neck

Allow access to fingers for checking circulation

SLING & SWATHE

Secure the sling with bandages across chest

Seek medical attention as soon as possible with _ANY_ broken bone

Examples of leg splints

Fold or roll pad as shown, out of foam or some other camp material

Folded

Rolled

Secure with tape, twine or belts

Check distal pulse (on top foot) frequently

Closed Fracture - skin & muscle intact

Open Fracture - skin broken, bone open to contamination

* <u>Do</u> <u>not</u> apply traction, cover wound & splint as is

Hypothermia

Signs & Symptoms:

Early

- Shivering begins
- Apathy
- Clumsiness
- Slurred speech
- Stiff fingers
- Stumbling
- Strange behavior

Late

- Obvious mental deterioration
- Incoherence
- Unconsciousness

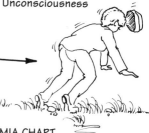

HYPOTHERMIA CHART
(In Water)

If the Water Temp. is (F.)...	Exhaustion or Unconsciousness	Expected Time of Survival Is...
32.5°	Under 15 Min.	Under 15-45 Min.
32.5°-40.0°	15-30 Mins.	30-90 Min.
40°-50°	30-60 Mins.	1-3 Hrs.
50°-60°	1-2 Hrs.	1-6 Hrs.
60°-70°	2-7 Hrs.	2-40 Hrs.
70°-80°	3-12 Hrs.	Indefinitely
Over-80°	Indefinitely	

Note: For <u>hypothermia</u> <u>danger</u> on land, refer to "Wind Chill" chart on page 100 of this section.

Treatment in Field:

Raise victim's body temperature with dry clothing, shelter, insulation (sleeping bag, blankets etc.) & applied heat (hot water bottles, your own warm body)

Caution! Be careful not to burn the skin with hot water. Give warm liquids to drink <u>only</u> if you are sure victim is conscious and can swallow.

Frostbite

<u>Frostbite</u> is the freezing of a part of the body, most often the nose, ears, cheeks, fingers, or toes.

<u>Causes</u> <u>of</u> <u>frostbite</u>:
- Cold stress
- Low temperatures
- Wind chill
- Moisture
- Poor insulation
- Tight-fitting clothing or boots
- Dehydration

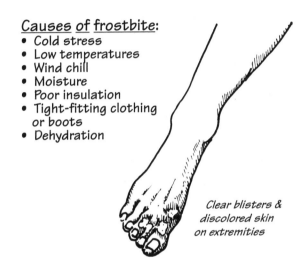

Clear blisters & discolored skin on extremities

Remove victim from cold exposure, remove clothing from affected body parts. If warm water is available, put parts in warm water until thawed & numbness decreases - Wrap parts in dry, clean gauze & seek medical attention as soon as possible. *<u>Do not rub</u>* affected areas!

Caution! Once you warm a body part you must keep it warm. If you cannot protect it from freezing again, it is better to leave it frozen until you can.

Heat-Related Emergencies

If <u>it</u> <u>is</u> <u>hot</u>, you may be the victim of *heat cramps*, *heat exhaustion* or, in extreme cases, *heat stroke*.

(Note: An ounce of prevention is worth a pound of cure - drink plenty of liquids to <u>avoid</u> heat-related emergencies.)

HEAT CRAMPS: These are the least serious, & usually occur in the leg muscles due to loss of body salts from heavy perspiration - Move to a cool place, rest affected muscle & drink water (cold water if available).

HEAT EXHAUSTION: <u>This</u> <u>can</u> <u>become</u> <u>serious</u> & is indicated by cold, clammy skin, slightly elevated temperature & possibly loss of consciousness - Move immediately to cool place & elevate legs, give cool water, and seek medical attention ASAP.

HEAT STROKE: This is the most serious heat-related problem, & the typical symptoms are hot, dry or wet skin, 105° temperature or higher, usually loss of consciousness - Move immediately to cool place & elevate head & shoulders. After victim is cooled, transport immediately to nearest medical facility - *Heat stroke is life-threatening!*

Caution! Be careful <u>not</u> to give liquids orally if victim is unconscious or cannot swallow.

Burns

Most burns in the field are *thermal (heat) burns,* caused by fire, over-exposure to sunlight, certain chemicals & hot surfaces or substances.

<u>Note</u>: If clothes catch on fire, STOP-DROP-ROLL.

STOP   DROP   ROLL

Hunting partner can assist by smothering with blankets, sleeping bags, etc.

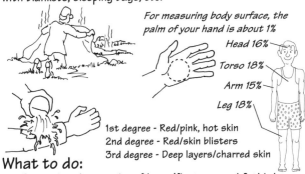

For measuring body surface, the palm of your hand is about 1%

Head 16%
Torso 18%
Arm 15%
Leg 18%

1st degree - Red/pink, hot skin
2nd degree - Red/skin blisters
3rd degree - Deep layers/charred skin

What to do:
- Determine the severity of burn (first, second & third degree burns increase in amount of skin layers destroyed)
- Remove clothing from burned area (if burns aren't severe)
- Douse with cool water until pain stops
- Cover with dry, nonstick, sterile dressing, keep area clean
- <u>*Watch*</u> for signs of infection & dehydration
- If burn is over *more than 15%* of body, or appears to be deep (second or third degree) - seek medical attention ASAP

Do <u>not</u>:
- Apply ice
- Break any blisters if it can be avoided
- Apply any type of salve, ointment, sprays or creams
- Pull or cut away clothing around deep burns

Sudden Illness

Chest pains/heart attack!

What to look for:

- Uncomfortable pressure, squeezing, or pain in center of chest that lasts more than a few minutes or comes & goes
- Pain spreading to the shoulders, neck, or arms
- Light-headedness, fainting, sweating, nausea, or shortness of breath

What to do:

Help victim get comfortable - usually sitting up, with back support, padding under the knees - loosen any tight clothing & be calm & reassuring - give nitroglycerin if the victim has any

CALL LOCAL EMS OR TRANSPORT VICTIM TO NEAREST
MEDICAL FACILITY AS SOON AS POSSIBLE

Moving a Victim: *Can be done in a variety of ways, some of which are shown here*

Do not:
- Make injury worse by moving victim
- Move a victim with spinal injury
- Leave unconscious victim alone
- Move victim without stabilizing the injured part

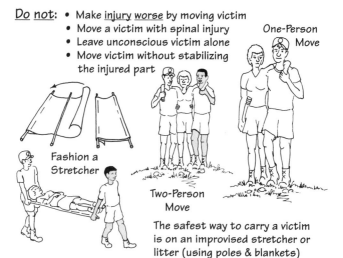

One-Person Move

Fashion a Stretcher

Two-Person Move

The safest way to carry a victim is on an improvised stretcher or litter (using poles & blankets)

Animal Bites

Very rare in the field. But if you are bitten & skin is broken, wash wound with soap & water. Apply pressure to control bleeding.

If the attack was unprovoked, consider the possibility of rabies. Notify authorities as soon as possible. Seek medical attention if needed.

Snake Bites

If snake is identified as venomous, <u>keep victim calm</u>. Keep the bitten arm or leg below heart level. Clean bite site with soap & water. Keep victim from ambulating, if possible. Immediately transport to nearest medical facility!

Insect Stings or Spider Bites

What to do:

If stung by bee or wasp, all you usually have to do is wash area with soap & water, apply cold pack for 15-20 minutes, relieve pain with aspirin or other pain reliever, & relieve itching with a cortisone cream

<u>Note</u>: If victim is known to have allergic reactions to insect stings - *seek medical attention immediately!* Antihistimines, such as benydryl, can relieve allergic reactions

Shiny black with red hour-glass shape on lower abdomen

Black Widow

If bitten by a venomous spider, such as the Black Widow or Brown Recluse, or even stung by a scorpion, clean bite or sting with soap & water & apply cold pack. Seek medical attention as soon as possible with any bite or sting!

Brown Recluse

Thin, brownish spider with a violin-shaped mark on top of head

Scorpion

Stinger

OUTDOORLIFE

Hunting Editor Jim Zumbo on:

How to Stay Warm Outdoors

- In extremely cold temperatures avoid perspiration at all costs, since moist undergarments will quickly chill your body. If you intend to walk or hike to a stand or blind where you will remain stationary, it's a good idea to remove any extra clothing until you get to the site. Use a day pack or carry the clothes. This way you will perspire much less (if at all) and be much more comfortable once you get on stand.

- If you are standing or sitting on the cold ground, always put some kind of cushioning insulation between your feet or backside and the ground. Cold quickly transfers from the ground to your body if you are in direct contact.

- On cold nights, when camping in a tent or structure where there is no heat, always put a foam cushion underneath your sleeping bag. Regardless of the amount of loft or the warmth rating your sleeping bag has, your body will compress the bag beneath you. This eliminates the loft, which provides a warm air layer that keeps you warm. If you don't have a foam mat, use articles of clothing or even newspapers between yourself and the ground. This insulation factor is especially necessary if you are sleeping on a cot; cold air circulates under the cot and will quickly chill you.

- Wool is a top choice for cold temperatures, but it does not effectively stop a strong wind. If you wear wool, you should be sure to wear some type of wind-resistant over-garment as well. Remember that strong wind during cold weather greatly increases your chance of becoming very cold.

- Insulated boots aren't everything they're cracked up to be. Many boots are rated to a certain temperature level, but those ratings are true only when you are moving constantly. If you intend to stand hunt, it's a good idea to jog in place for a few minutes to warm your feet. Another tip is to break your boots in well before going hunting. Poorly fitting boots will make your feet much colder. This happens because the boots may contain air pockets that break the effectiveness of the insulating layers.

- If you're riding a horse in cold weather you might think heat from the horse's body will keep you warm, but it doesn't work that way. Your body is separated from the horse by saddle blankets and the saddle. The best way to keep warm while riding on a horse is to get off and walk frequently, especially when you are going downhill. Not only will this warm you up, but it will also give the horse a break.

- Your hands commonly become very cold before other parts of your body do. This can happen because of improper gloves or gloves that are too light for the temperature. Wear insulated gloves or heavy-duty mittens. A good tip is to manipulate your fingers frequently to keep the circulation flowing.

- Keeping your head covered greatly increases your body warmth, since most body heat escapes via the head. Wear a waterproof/windproof hat, preferably a watch cap or balaclava that can be pulled down to protect your ears and face.

Wildlife

- Learn about wildlife and their habitat.
- Understand the needs of wildlife in relation to the needs of people.
- Understand how human decisions affect wildlife and how wildlife-related decisions are made.
- Know the different management tools used with wildlife and understand how they work.
- Know who is involved in wildlife-related decisions and how their influence affects wildlife.
- Understand your hunting heritage.
- Be involved and be a conservationist.

Wilderness Ecosystems

EVERGREEN WOODLANDS OF THE U.S.
• bald eagle • red squirrel • elk • black bear • raccoon • bobcat • turkey
• pileated woodpecker • Northern cardinal • porcupine • mule deer

BROADLEAF WOODLANDS OF THE U.S.

• red fox • screech owl • whitetail deer • raccoon
• copperhead snake • fox squirrel • yellow-bellied sapsucker
• tree frog • ruffed grouse • Eastern cottontail rabbit • red bat
• long-tailed weasel • opossum • Eastern chipmunk

DESERT AREAS OF THE U.S.

• red-tailed hawk • kit fox • collared peccary
• diamond-backed rattlesnake • kangaroo rat • collared lizard
• turkey vulture • desert bighorn sheep • Gambel's quail
• spotted skunk • roadrunner • cactus wren • horned lizard

WETLAND AREAS OF THE U.S.
• osprey • red-winged blackbird • great blue heron
• black-crowned night-heron • damselfly
• dragonfly • water snake • Northern harrier • mallard duck
• pintail duck • mink • snapping turtle • bull frog

PRAIRIE AREAS OF THE U.S.

• turkey vulture • bison • badger • Western meadowlark • prairie rattlesnake
• burrowing owl • red-tailed hawk • pronghorn antelope
• coyote • prairie dog • black-tailed jackrabbit • sage grouse

AGRICULTURAL AREAS OF THE U.S.

• ring-necked pheasant • yellow-headed blackbird • bobwhite quail
• cottontail rabbit • sandhill crane • pintail ducks
• gray partridge • admiral butterfly • gray fox

SUBURBAN AREAS OF THE U.S.
• Eastern bluebird • bluejay • raccoon • boat-tailed grackle
• American robin • common flicker • monarch butterfly • coyote
• Eastern chipmunk • gray squirrel • box turtle • American toad

America is losing wildlife habitat to various causes each year. This creates an urgency for better stewardship and conservation of the forests, wetlands, streams and rivers that we still have to enjoy for outdoor activities such as hunting and camping.

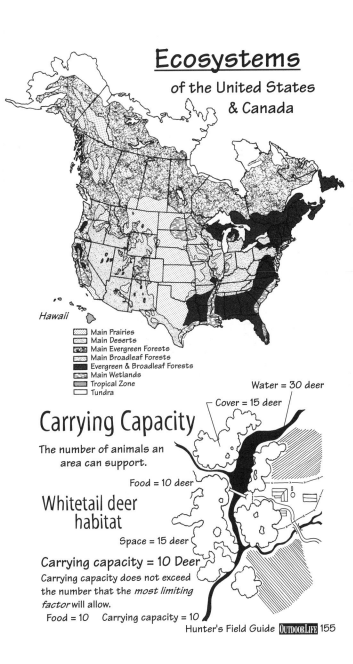

Ecosystems

of the United States & Canada

Hawaii

- Main Prairies
- Main Deserts
- Main Evergreen Forests
- Main Broadleaf Forests
- Evergreen & Broadleaf Forests
- Main Wetlands
- Tropical Zone
- Tundra

Water = 30 deer

Cover = 15 deer

Carrying Capacity

The number of animals an area can support.

Food = 10 deer

Whitetail deer habitat

Space = 15 deer

Carrying capacity = 10 Deer

Carrying capacity does not exceed the number that the *most limiting factor* will allow.

Food = 10   Carrying capacity = 10

COMMON WILDLIFE SIGNS

WILDLIFE SIGNS	Feeding Sign	Trails & Tracks	Shelter	Body Waste & Castoffs	Other Sign
Whitetail Deer	Browse line		Woods & brush	Scat	Scrape
Elk	Cropped grass & brush		Mountain forests	Scat	Shed antlers
Mule Deer	Cropped browse		Brushy valleys, plateaus	Scat	Antler rub
Black Bear	Stripped bark		Rock shelters	Scat	Deep claw marks
Pronghorn Antelope	Cropped sage & browse		Brushy draws	Scat	Bedding area

COMMON WILDLIFE SIGNS

WILDLIFE SIGNS	Feeding Sign	Trails & Tracks	Shelter	Body Waste & Castoffs	Other Sign
Bighorn Sheep	Cropped grasses & herbs		Rocky outcrops, ledges	Scat	Broken cacti & twigs
Coyote	Broken eggs, bones		Dugouts & brush.	Scat	Teeth marks on melons
Cottontail Rabbit	Nibbling on grass & leaves		Brush, logs & old holes	Scat	Bedded area in tall grass
Fox Squirrel	Gnawed acorns & nuts		Holes in hollow trees	Scat	Trail on bark to hollow
Wild Turkey	Scratch marks in leaves		Nest in brush	Scat	Oval dust bath

Wildlife Habitat Components

Food

Browsers — Brush

Grazers — Grass

Predators — Meat

Water

Streams & Rivers

Ponds & Lakes

Springs & Seeps & Vegetation

Cover

Thermal Cover

Nesting Cover

Escape Cover

Space

Open Country

Hunting and feeding areas

Migration Corridors

Arrangement
of Habitat

Wide sagebrush
flats, ringed
by heavy
timber

Open meadows
surrounded by thick
timber & brambles

Sagebrush &
meadows
mottled with
timber, seeps
& springs

Thick overgrown
timber & tangles
dotted by meadows

Wildlife Populations
Limiting Factors
(What limits population growth)

Starvation

Disease/Parasites

Accidents

Natural Factors
(fires, floods, etc. . .)

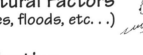

Hunting
(minimal effect
on game animals)

Predation

Other

Natural factors affecting
Wildlife Habitat
that are <u>positive</u> or <u>negative</u>

Fires

- Animals could get burned
- Food & cover burned
- Water source may evaporate
+ Regrowth of nutritional vegetation
+ Encourages grass cover
+ Cleans out debris

Extreme Cold

- Younger or weaker animals die
- There may be fewer animals born
- Takes more energy just to survive

Heavy Snow

Drought

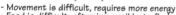

- Movement is difficult, requires more energy
- Food is difficult, often impossible, to find
- Thermal cover is difficult to reach & often ineffective
+ Insulates plants & animals from extreme cold

- Vegetation withers, food disappears
- Water sources dry up
- Cover thins

Flood

Over-population

- Habitat & wildlife washed away or inundated.
- Vegetation drowns
+ Disperses seeds & soil

- Crowding and trampling of vegetation
- Disease spreads easily
- Vegetation is stripped

Habitat loss...
How bad is it?

Wetlands:

More than half of America's waterfowl and wildlife areas have been drained and/or plowed.

Streams and Rivers:

In 1992, 38 states issued warnings about eating fish from their rivers and streams. In 1995, 48 states issued warnings about fish and nine states warned about waterfowl, due to danger of eating those that might be contaminated with pesticides or metals.

The Land:

In the West, most of the major cities have more than doubled in size in the last 20 years.

America is losing more habitat yearly.

WETLANDS DRAINED
for agricultural use
or other development

States losing more than 50% of wetlands in last 200 years

Other states with significant losses of wetlands in last 25 years

Wildlife Populations-Annual Cycles

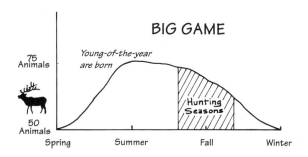

BIG GAME

75 Animals

Young-of-the-year are born

Hunting Seasons

50 Animals

Spring   Summer   Fall   Winter

SMALL GAME

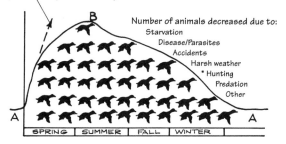

Unrestricted production (if no limiting factors exist)

B

Number of animals decreased due to:
Starvation
Disease/Parasites
Accidents
Harsh weather
* Hunting
Predation
Other

A

A

SPRING | SUMMER | FALL | WINTER

A   Annual breeding stock

B   Average yearly production or biotic potential

*   In most cases, hunters take some of the animals from the annual surplus that would be lost anyway.

Carrying capacity of the land increases in early summer when there is a lot of food and cover. This healthy habitat is soon filled by the new broods of birds. In late summer, when the population and the available food and cover reach their peaks, some birds begin to die.

The Ups & Downs of Wildlife Populations

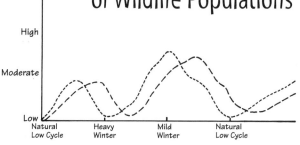

High

Moderate

Low

| Natural Low Cycle | Heavy Winter | Mild Winter | Natural Low Cycle |

- - - - Key Habitat factors - Rabbit: Climate and food and natural cycle
— — — Key Habitat factors - Coyote: food and climate

Number-one Threat to Wildlife

POLLUTION

URBAN DEVELOPMENT

OUTDOOR RECREATION

OVERGRAZING

NATURAL RESOURCE DEVELOPMENT

NATURAL DISASTERS

HABITAT

Enemies no more

Human development and wildlife needs are often at odds. It doesn't have to be that way.

Habitat Loss

We should work together to protect our world for

wildlife & people

Urban development:

Planners and developers can build in greenbelts and habitat corridors that will allow wildlife to use existing blocks of habitat more effectively.

Mining and oil:

By taking proper steps at the opening of a mine or drilling a well, habitat loss can be reduced and habitat can be restored when the mine is closed or the well capped.

Ranching and farming:

Ranchers can practice low-impact grazing techniques and proper grazing management. Farmers can monitor pesticide use and capture and treat runoff before it contaminates habitat. Both ranchers and farmers can use water conservation techniques.

Pollution:

Cities can treat and recycle waste-water and many solid wastes. Factories and industries can treat water and air to remove pollutants before they leave the site and escape into the water we drink and the air we breathe.

Every Citizen:

Should become informed about local wildlife habitat issues. Recycle and dispose of pollutants properly, and practice good water conservation.

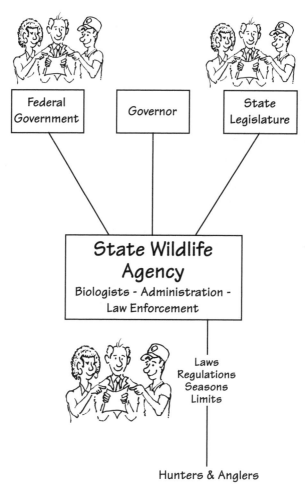

How Wildlife Laws are made

Federal Government

Governor

State Legislature

State Wildlife Agency
Biologists - Administration - Law Enforcement

Laws
Regulations
Seasons
Limits

Hunters & Anglers

How Wildlife Decisions are made

WILDLIFE BUILDING — DECISION MAKERS

WILDLIFE LOBBY

Wildlife Agencies

have the interest of wildlife as their goal, but often must work with conflicting interests and different political viewpoints.

Planning & Zoning Commissions

do not always consider wildlife in their decisions. They must always consider economic, community, public service and municipal factors in planning and zoning. With good planning, these are compatible with wildlife interests.

Land Managers

include wildlife as part of their programs, but must consider the many other uses of public land.

Park Managers & Commissioners

Wildlife is a component of most state, national and local parks. Park philosophies differ, and wildlife considerations can take a second-seat to human convenience and comfort.

Private Land Owners

usually have an economic interest in the use of their land. If wildlife is not a part of that interest, it often suffers. If wildlife is a part of that interest, it will benefit. "If wildlife pays, it stays."

Wildlife can't speak for itself...
we must be the ones to speak up

Keep Informed: Read the papers, subscribe to hotlines and talk to those in the know. Study the impacts of pending decisions.

Be Involved: Attend meetings, get to know the people responsible for decisions and become a positive, persistant force.

Follow-up: When decision-makers decide to benefit wildlife, let them know what great choices they made.

Tools of Wildlife
Management

Habitat Protection

Acquisition of key habitat areas to provide wildlife habitat into the future.

Habitat Enhancement

Working with landowners to encourage the manipulation of vegetation by burning, controlled grazing, brush control and seeding to provide better food and cover for wildlife.

Surveys & Studies

Estimating populations and how they're doing, surveys are used in setting limits and seasons.

Hunting Laws

Wildlife laws, including game laws, have done much to protect wildlife and the hunting privilege. Game laws provide for:
- Public Safety
- Protecting wildlife
- Sharing wildlife equally

Hunting & Trapping

In many areas the human predator has stepped in to fill the niche left by the disappearance of wild predators. More importantly, hunters support wildlife management with money, time and work.

HUNTING
SEASON
OPEN

Trap and Transplant

Captured in one area and released in suitable habitat elsewhere

Exotic and Strange

Some animals were introduced inadvertently—such as starlings, grackles and crows—following human development across barriers such as the Great Plains, Rocky Mountains and Great Basin. Now they're found across North America.

Some exotics—such as axis deer, black buck antelope, fallow deer, carp, brown trout and ring-necked pheasant—were introduced intentionally. They quickly adapted to their new home and now often out-compete native wild animals.

Many introduced exotics don't do well in new habitat. Sometimes they do very well, and may provide food, recreation or research for humans. Exotics can cause problems for native wildlife.

Exotics can:

- Spread disease
- Out-compete native wildlife
- Over-run habitat
- Inter-breed
- Die out

As a result, North American states, provinces and territories have strict import-export and _possession of wildlife_ laws.

The Changing Tradition of Hunting

Stone Age humans hunted for food, using stones and clubs as hunting tools. The first technology was probably hunting technology.

Very soon after the invention of firearms people saw their use for hunting. As ignition and aiming became more reliable, hunter success improved.

Hunting was an essential part of pioneer life. The use of firearms was essential to survival in the remote and isolated regions of the continent.

Today, hunting continues the tradition. Few people rely on hunting for survival. Hunting offers the chance to renew our ties with our heritage and to make a connection with the natural world.

A wildlife management success story: Un-Endangered Species

During the early 1900s, the future of many American species of wildlife was in question. Destruction of habitat and commercial exploitation had reduced populations to critical levels. Contrary to popular opinion, hunters were not the cause of this decline. In fact, according to conservation experts, it was the excise taxes and license fees imposed on sportsmen of this country that largely paid for programs that helped rescue many species from extinction. The following shows just how successful sportsmen have been at helping wildlife.

Canada Goose

THEN 1,100,000
Habitat destruction reduced Canada goose populations to a low of some 1,100,000 in the late 1940's. Today, there are about twice that number as a result of wildlife management measures implemented by the nation's conservation agencies.
NOW 3,760,000*

Trumpeter Swan

THEN 73
In 1935, only 73 trumpeter swans were known to exist in the United States. ** Today, there are some 900 in several national parks and wildlife refuges.
NOW 900*

**In the lower 48 states

* Source: National Shooting Sports Foundation, 1996

Wild Turkey

THEN 100,000
While records of turkey populations during the early 1900's are vague, estimates are that encroaching civilization and habitat loss may have reduced populations to 100,000 birds or less. Today, conservation programs have restored turkeys to sustainable levels in 49 states with a total population of some 4,500,000 birds
NOW 4,500,000*

Whitetail Deer

THEN 500,000
In 1900, an official U.S. survey estimated less than 500,000 whitetail deer remaining in the nation. Today, there are about 18 million.
NOW 18,000,000*

Rocky Mountain Elk

THEN 41,000
In 1907, only 41,000 elk could be counted throughout the United States. Today, there are more than 800,000. Most western states now have surplus populations that may be hunted during regulated seasons.
NOW 800,000*

Pronghorn Antelope

THEN 12,000
About 50 years ago, the total United States population of pronghorn antelope was only about 12,000. Today, habitat restoration and restocking programs have helped increase pronghorn populations to more than 1,100,000.
NOW 1,100,000*

Paying for Wildlife

- Hunters pay millions of dollars in license and tag fees that pay for wildlife management.
- Hunters have sponsored legislation that has created conservation stamps and funds to protect and enhance wildlife habitat.
- Through organizations such as Whitetails Unlimited, Pheasants Forever, Rocky Mountain Elk Foundation, National Wild Turkey Federation, Quail Unlimited, the Mule Deer Foundation, Ducks Unlimited and other conservation groups, hunters have raised millions of dollars and contributed thousands of hours to benefit wildlife.

HUNTERS

Do you know that you have contributed over $5.5 BILLION for conservation in less than 60 years?

That you annually pay over $372 MILLION a year for conservation?

That you do more to aid wildlife than any other group in America?

Many people would support hunting more if they knew who was picking up the bills for conservation — *hunters*.

You contribute...

every time you buy a federal duck stamp. How? The money paid by hunters for these stamps is used by the government to buy and lease wetlands for waterfowl refuges and waterfowl production. Many different varieties of shorebirds and animals which are not hunted share the benefits with those that are hunted. Through the purchase of federal duck stamps, hunters presently spend about $11 million a year for conservation.

You contribute...

every time you buy a new gun or box of ammunition or archery equipment. How? Because when the Pittman-Robertson Act of 1937 was passed with strong hunter support, it specified that an 11 percent excise tax on sporting arms and ammunition was to be spent for conservation. The money you pay under this act is distributed to the states, enabling them to set aside and improve land for wildlife. This land, paid for by hunters, is enjoyed by all the public. Hunters provide almost $86 million a year for conservation through this excise tax, which, since 1937, has raised over $2 billion.

You contribute...

every time you buy a hunting license. How? You support state fish and wildlife agencies, which are responsible for managing fish and wildlife. Hunters' license fees currently provide state wildlife departments with over $185 million a year. License buyers have aided conservation efforts by over $2.3 billion.

Hunters as
Conservationists

- Hunters were the first conservationists in America -
  - Teddy Roosevelt established the first national parks, developed conservation programs and started the wildlife preserve program.
  - Other early conservationists joined Roosevelt to start the Boone and Crockett Club, one of the first conservation groups in the world.
- Key Conservationists, such as Roosevelt and Aldo Leopold, were hunters -
  - Conservationists enjoyed hunting and understood its place in wildlife management.
  - Conservation groups flourished on the national and local level during the 1920's-30's and 40's. They were primarily composed of hunters.
  - Hunters led the way in the restoration of America's wildlife.
- Hunters still lead the way in conservation -
  - Millions of people hunt and also contribute to the welfare of wildlife in America.
  - Responsible hunters belong to wildlife groups and actively contribute time, money and effort.
  - You should seek out and join the wildlife organization where you feel you can contribute the most to wildlife.

OUTDOORLIFE

Hunting Editor Jim Zumbo on:

Deer-Hunting Tips for Various Habitats

Evergreen Forests

Most forests have very little forage for deer because sunlight is prevented from reaching the forest floor. Deer often use the forest as security cover and hide there during the day, but they normally travel out of the forests in late afternoon, seeking food elsewhere. Since deer prefer to eat brush that grows best in the open, set up a ground blind near potential feeding areas. Pick an area that offers good visibility and stay there until shooting light is over, as that's when deer are most active.

Hardwood Forests

Look for signs of deer activity such as well-used trails, scrapes and rubs. Find a spot where you can watch those clues, preferably where you have good visibility. If other hunters share the woods, stay at your vantage point as long as possible to intercept deer trying to avoid other people. Try stillhunting by moving very slowly, stopping, looking and listening. Always keep the wind in your face so animals don't get your scent.

Agricultural Areas

Deer feed extensively in fields during the night but leave them as it gets light in the morning. They spend the rest of the day in heavy cover, often very close to the fields. A good strategy is to set up a tree stand or ground blind where you can watch travel lanes between feeding and bedding areas. These will be used in early-morning and late-afternoon hours. During the day, walk slowly through thickets with a partner walking parallel to you. It's often possible to push deer to each other.

Desert

Dry areas typically contain sparse forage, so animals often cover much more ground when feeding. Find a vantage point from which you can see a long distance, and use binoculars or a spotting scope to watch for deer. Since desert regions often have plenty of roads and good access, hike as far as you can from your vehicle to get away from other hunters. Walk to

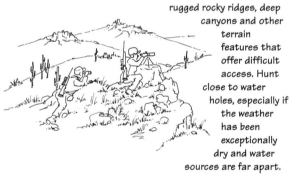

rugged rocky ridges, deep canyons and other terrain features that offer difficult access. Hunt close to water holes, especially if the weather has been exceptionally dry and water sources are far apart.

Brushy Terrain

Since deer feed and bed in brush, a good way to see them in this dense vegetation is to put on a drive with other hunters. Choose standers and blockers, positioning standers in spots where deer are likely to run out. These may be along saddles and trails that are frequently used by animals. Drivers should carefully work through the brush, zigzagging about to confuse the deer. Be sure that all hunters are wearing hunter-orange clothing for safety reasons, and that all hunters are cautioned to pick shots carefully because of the concentration of people in one area.

Planning the Hunt

Filing the trip plan.

Sample Trip Plan

Trip plan of _____

Date & Time of Departure: _____

Date & Time of Return:_____

Destination: _____

Who Will Go Along: _____

_____

Route Taken:_____

_____

_____

Route Returning: _____

_____

_____

Permits Required :_____

_____

Special Equipment Needs:_____

_____

Special Clothing Needs:_____

_____

<u>Note</u>: *If traveling to remote hunt area, attach a detailed map with travel routes marked.*

File the trip plan with:

- At least two responsible adults
- Local authority (sheriff or ranger) in remote areas

<u>Preparation</u> & <u>Packing Up</u>

Checklist:

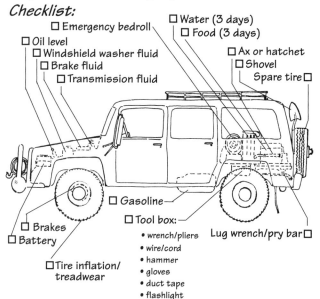

☐ Emergency bedroll
☐ Water (3 days)
☐ Food (3 days)
☐ Oil level
☐ Windshield washer fluid
☐ Brake fluid
☐ Transmission fluid
☐ Ax or hatchet
☐ Shovel
Spare tire ☐
☐ Gasoline
☐ Tool box:
  • wrench/pliers
  • wire/cord
  • hammer
  • gloves
  • duct tape
  • flashlight
☐ Brakes
☐ Battery
☐ Tire inflation/treadwear
Lug wrench/pry bar ☐

Don't forget your maps!

MAPS SHOW:

- Roads, trails, & access to your hunting area
- Sources of potential water, food, & cover for wildlife
- Barriers to cross while hunting
- Barriers to wildlife (which can be used to your advantage)
- Terrain to prepare for
- Elevations to prepare for
- Potential campsites
- Likely travel routes for wildlife
- Public and private lands

Field <u>Scouting</u>

Your first *REAL* hunt of the season!

GET TO KNOW YOUR HUNT AREA!

- Look for the easiest, safest routes
- Watch for obstacles, (streams, cliffs, ravines, etc.)
- Check out camping spots, rest areas, facilities & roads
- Note location of houses, farm buildings, highways

Often overlooked in the scouting process is getting to *know the people* in your hunt area.

- Get on a first-name basis with people in the area
- Ask about wildlife, weather, terrain & access
- Note the human patterns such as school bus stops, rancher checking his livestock, etc.
- Make local contacts to check conditions just prior to your hunt
- Obtain permission to retrieve game on adjacent land

Conduct your scouting just like a hunt.

- Survey the area as close to the time of your actual hunt as is possible
- Look for tracks, scat, dusting & wallow areas, rubs & scrapes
- Note well-used game trails, feeding & watering areas
- Watch for other wildlife that use your hunt area

Maps

Use your topo-graphic (topo) map & graph paper to plot an altitude chart. Then you can "see" the type of climbs you face.

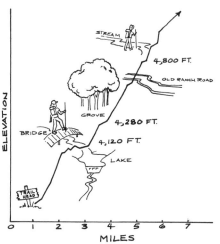

Maps are helpful in all phases of *pre-scouting*, to determine your needs in preparation for the hunt.

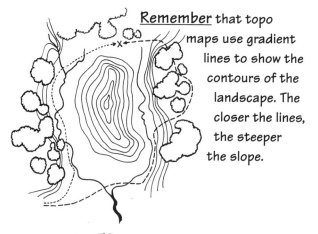

Remember that topo maps use gradient lines to show the contours of the landscape. The closer the lines, the steeper the slope.

Refer to <u>page 79</u> in the "Hunting Responsibilities" chapter, to learn how to read a topographic map.

The Hunt - <u>Fair Chase</u>

Fair Chase, as defined by the Boone & Crockett Club, is the ethical, sportsmanlike, & lawful pursuit & taking of any free-ranging wild animal in a manner that does not give the hunter an improper or unfair advantage over such game animals.

Use of any of the following methods in the taking of game is considered *Unfair Chase*:

- Spotting or herding game from the air, then landing, pursuing, & shooting
- Herding, pursuing, or shooting game from motor boat or motor vehicle
- Use of *illegal* electronic devices for attracting, locating, or observing game, or for guiding hunter to such game (check state & provincial laws)
- Hunting game confined by fences or enclosures, or game transplanted solely for the purpose of commercial shooting
- Taking game illegally or using illegal methods against regulations of the federal government or any state, province, territory or tribal lands

Always Remember . . . . . .

- show respect to landowners & managers
- respect wildlife
- obey wildlife laws
- respect the land
- be courteous to other hunters
- be courteous to those who don't hunt

<u>Don't</u> .....
take these shots

At an animal moving over a hill, or at its rear end.

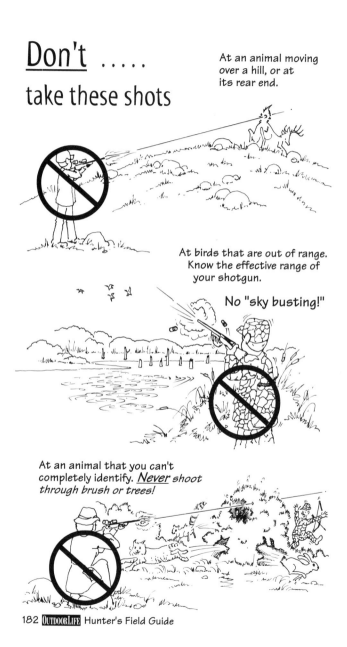

At birds that are out of range. Know the effective range of your shotgun.

No "sky busting!"

At an animal that you can't completely identify. *Never* shoot through brush or trees!

Ask Yourself . . . . .

Is it legal? Is it right? Is it safe?

Fair chase allows the hunter to pursue game, using hunting skills, knowledge of wildlife & outdoor savvy, without putting the game animal at an unfair disadvantage. Below are examples of what is considered fair and unfair hunting practice for just one species.

FAIR - Using decoys & calls to hunt turkeys

UNFAIR - And/or <u>illegal</u> - shooting the turkey out of the roost tree

<u>Know the rules</u> and abide by them! It always makes for a more enjoyable and satisfying hunt!

Remember . . . . .
It's <u>YOUR</u> responsibility to be safe & ethical!

If you use dogs in hunting ——

- Know & follow all regulations & laws regarding dogs & hunting
- Properly & completely train your dog for the specific game
- *Control your dog* in the field at all times
- Properly care for your animals in camp & in the field

If you use ATVs during your hunt -

- Wear a helmet & protective glasses
- Wear sturdy, high boots
- Don't chase wildlife
- Take care of the landscape

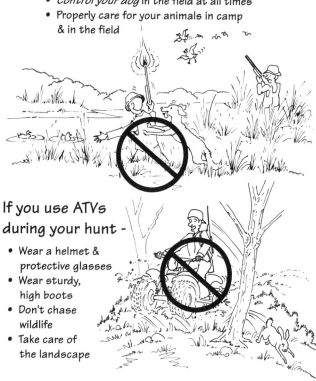

Remember . . . . .
When tracking & locating game

<u>Trackers</u> & <u>flankers</u> -

Keep 50 yards
apart, with tracker
concentrating
on trail,
while flankers look
ahead for downed
or fleeing
game

Approach downed wildlife carefully ——

- Approach from behind quietly
- Wait for a few minutes & watch for movement
  - Poke animal gently with a stick
  - Touch the eye gently, if there's no reaction animal is usually dead

Refer to pages 39-40 in the "Archery" chapter for more about tracking.

Finding Places to Hunt

Contact the following for maps, information, etc.

Dept. of Agriculture -
U. S. Forest Service
P. O. Box 96090
Washington, D.C. 20090

States -
Depts. of Transportation
Wildlife Departments
Tourism Departments
State Parks

County Offices -
Assessor's Office
Planner's Office

Dept. of the Interior -
Bureau of Land Management
1849 C Street, NW Rm. 5600
Washington D.C. 20240

National Park Service
Interior Bldg.
P. O. Box 37127
Washington D.C. 20013-7127

U.S. Geological Survey (East)
National Center
Reston, VA 22092

U.S. Geological Survey (West)
P. O. Box 25286
Denver, CO 80225

*You may also contact the
state or provincial Hunter
Education Coordinator offices
listed on the following pages.*

United States

ALABAMA

Dept. of Conserv. & Natural Res.
64 North Union St.
Montgomery, AL 36130-1457

ALASKA

Division of Fish & Game
333 Raspberry Rd.
Anchorage, AL 99518-1599

ARIZONA

Az. Game & Fish Dept.
2221 West Greenway Rd.
Phoenix, AZ 85023

ARKANSAS

Ark. Game & Fish Comm.
#2 Natural Resources Dr.
Little Rock, AR 72205

CALIFORNIA

Dept. of Fish & Game
1416 9th St., Rm. 1342-1
Sacramento, CA 95814

COLORADO

Division of Wildlife
6060 Broadway
Denver, CO 80216

CONNECTICUT

Franklin WMA
391 Route 32
North Franklin, CT 06254

Sessions Wood WMA
P.O. Box 1550
Burlington, CT 06013

DELAWARE

Division of Fish & Wildlife
89 Kings Hwy.
P. O. Box 1401
Dover, DE 19903

FLORIDA

Game & Fresh Water Fish Comm.
Farris Bryant Bldg.
620 S. Meridian St.
Talahassee, FL 32399-1600

GEORGIA

DNR/Wildlife Res. Div.
2070 US Hwy. 278 SE
Social Circle, GA 30279

HAWAII

1130 N. Nimitz Hwy. #B-299
Honolulu, Hil 96817-4521

64-1035 Mamalahoa Hwy. Ste. D
Kamuela, HI 96743

IDAHO

Fish & Game Dept.
600 S. Walnut St., P. O. Box 25
Boise, ID 83707

ILLINOIS

Illinois DNR/Div. of Ed.
524 S. 2nd St.
Springfield, Il. 62701-1787

INDIANA

Dept. of Natural Resources
402 W. Washington St., W-255D
Indianapolis, IN 46204

IOWA

Dept. of Natural Resources
Wallace State Office Bldg.
Des Moines, IA 50319-0034

KANSAS

Kansas Dept. of Wildlife & Parks
512 SE 25th Ave.
Pratt, KS 67124

KENTUCKY

Dept. of Fish & Wildlife Res.
#1 Game Farm Rd.
Frankfort, KY 40601

LOUISIANA

Dept. of Wildlife & Fisheries
1995 Shreveport Hwy.
Pineville, LA 71360

MAINE

Dept. of Inland Fisheries & Wildlife
284 State St. Station 41
Augusta, ME 04333

MARYLAND

Md. Natural Resources Police
580 Taylor Ave.
Annapolis, MD 21401

MASSACHUSETTS

Hunter Ed./Enforcement
P. O. Box 408
Westminster, MA 01473-0408

MICHIGAN

Dept. of Natural Resources
P.O. Box 30031
530 W. Allegan
Lansing, MI 48909

MINNESOTA

Dept. of Natural Resources
500 Lafayette Rd., Box 47
St. Paul, MN 55155-4047

Dept. of Natural Resources
500 Lafayette Rd., Box 47
St. Paul, MN 55155-4047

MISSISSIPPI

Dept. of Wildlife, Fisheries & Parks
P. O. Box 451
Jackson, MS 39205-0451

MISSOURI

Dept. of Conservation
P.O. 180
2901 W. Truman Blvd.
Jefferson City, MO 65102-0180

MONTANA

Montana Fish, Wildlife & Parks
1420 E. 6th Ave.
P.O. Box 200701
Helena, MT 59620

NEBRASKA

AK-SAR-BEN Aquarium
21502 W. Hwy. 31
Gretna, NE 68028

NEVADA

Division of Wildlife
1100 Valley Rd.
Reno, NV 89512

NEW HAMPSHIRE

Fish & Game Dept.
2 Hazen Dr.
Concord, NH 03301

NEW JERSEY

NJ Div. of Fish, Game & Wildlife
Rt. 26, 173 W.
Hampton, NJ 08827

NEW MEXICO

Dept. of Game & Fish
3841 Midway Place NE
Albuquerque, NM 87109

NEW YORK

Fish & Wildlife/Env. Cons.
50 Wolf Rd.
Albany, NY 12233-4800

NORTH CAROLINA

Wildlife Resource Comm./Enf. Div.
512 N. Salisbury St.
Raleigh, NC 27604

NORTH DAKOTA

Game & Fish Dept.
100 N. Bismark Expressway
Bismark, ND 58501

OHIO

OH Div. of Wildlife/Outdoor Skills
1840 Belcher Dr.
Columbus, OH 43224-1329

OH Div. of Wildlife
1840 Belcher Dr.
Columbus, OH 43224-1329

OKLAHOMA

Dept. of Wildlife Conservation
1801 N. Lincoln
Oklahoma City, OK 73105-4998

OREGON

OR. Dept. of Fish & Wildlife
P.O. Box 59
2501 SW 1st Ave.
Portland, OR 97201

OR. Dept. of Fish & Wildlife
P. O. Box 59
2501 SW 1st Ave.
Portland, OR 97201

PENNSYLVANIA

Game Comm./Hunter-Trapper Ed.
2001 Elmerton Ave.
Harrisburg, PA 17110-9797

RHODE ISLAND

RI Div. of Fish & Wildlife
4808 Tower Hill Rd.
Wakefield, RI 02879

SOUTH CAROLINA

Dept. of Natural Resources
Rembert C. Dennis Bldg.
1000 Assemble St., Box 167
Columbia, SC 29202

SOUTH DAKOTA

Dept. of Game, Fish & Parks
523 E. Capitol, Foss Bldg.
Pierre, SD 57501-3182

TENNESSEE

Wildlife Resource Agency
P.O. Box 40747
Ellington Ag. Ctr., Hogan Rd.
Nashville, TN 37204

TEXAS

Tx. Parks & Wildlife Dept.
4200 Smith School Rd.
Austin, TX 78744

UTAH

Utah Div. of Wildlife Resources
1596 W. North Temple
Salt Lake City, UT 84116

VERMONT

Dept. of Fish & Wildlife
103 S. Main St.
Waterbury, VT 05671-0501

VIRGINIA

Va. Dept. of Game & Inland Fish.
P.O. Box 11104
4010 W. Broad St.
Richmond, VA 23230

WASHINGTON

Dept. of Fish & Wildlife
600 Capitol Way N.
Olympia, WA 98501-1091

WEST VIRGINIA

DNR/ Law Enf. Section
Capitol Complex Bldg. 3
1900 Kanawha Blvd. E.
Charleston, WV 25305

WISCONSIN

Dept. of Natural Resources
P.O. 7921, 101 S. Webster
Madison, WI 53707

WYOMING

Game & Fish Dept.
5400 Bishop Blvd.
Cheyenne, WY 82006